Top Notes

T0360043

Anthony Doerr's
All the Light We Cannot See

Study notes for Common Module:
Texts and Human Experiences
2019–2023 HSC

Bruce Pattinson

A
FIVE SENSES
PUBLICATION

Five Senses Education Pty Ltd
2/195 Prospect Highway
Seven Hills 2147
New South Wales
Australia

Pattinson, Bruce
Top Notes – All the Light We Cannot See
ISBN 978-1-76032-219-9

CONTENTS

TOP NOTES SERIES

This series has been created to assist HSC students of English in their understanding of set texts. Top Notes are easy to read, providing analysis of issues and discussion of important ideas contained in the texts.

Particular care has been taken to ensure that students are able to examine each text in the context of the module it has been allocated to.

Each text generally includes:

- Notes on the specific module
- Plot summary
- Character analysis
- Setting
- Thematic concerns
- Language studies
- Essay questions and a modelled response
- Other textual material
- Study practice questions
- Useful quotes

We have covered the areas we feel are important for students in their study of *Texts and Human Experiences* for their Common Module. I am sure you will find these Top Notes useful in your studies of English.

Bruce Pattinson
Series Editor

COMMON MODULE:
TEXTS AND HUMAN EXPERIENCES

"It is quite possible—overwhelmingly probable, one might guess—that we will always learn more about human life and personality from novels than from scientific psychology"

NOAM CHOMSKY

What is the Common Module?

The Common Module set for the 2019–23 HSC is *Texts and Human Experiences*. It is compulsory to study this topic as prescribed by NESA and it is common to all three English courses. Remember: you will be learning how texts reveal individual and collective human experiences. There are no right or wrong answers in this module – it is about how you see and interpret material and engage with it.

In the Common Module you will be analysing one prescribed text and a range of short texts that are related to the idea of human experiences. You will analyse texts not only to investigate the ideas they present about this area but also how they convey these ideas. This means you will be looking closely at the techniques a composer uses to represent his / her messages and shape meaning. You will also be looking at relationships between texts in regard to the experiences you explore. Overall, you will become an expert on texts and the human experience — that is, the different notions people have about human experience and the various ways composers manipulate techniques to communicate their ideas about it.

Specifically you will look at one set text from the following list.

- Doerr, Anthony, *All the Light We Cannot See*
- Lohrey, Amanda, *Vertigo*
- Orwell, George, *Nineteen Eighty-Four*
- Parrett, Favel, *Past the Shallows*
- Dobson, Rosemary 'Young Girl at a Window', 'Over the Hill', 'Summer's End', 'The Conversation', 'Cock Crow', 'Amy Caroline', 'Canberra Morning'
- Slessor, Kenneth 'Wild Grapes', 'Gulliver', 'Out of Time', 'Vesper-Song of the Reverend Samuel Marsden', 'William Street', 'Beach Burial'
- Harrison, Jane, *Rainbow's End*
- Miller, Arthur, *The Crucible*
- Shakespeare, William, *The Merchant of Venice*
- Winton, Tim, *The Boy Behind the Curtain* Chapters: 'Havoc: A Life in Accidents', 'Betsy', 'Twice on Sundays', 'The Wait and the Flow', 'In the Shadow of the Hospital', 'The Demon Shark', 'Barefoot in the Temple of Art'
- Yousafzai, Malala & Lamb, Christina, *I am Malala*
- Daldry, Stephen, *Billy Elliot*
- O'Mahoney, Ivan, *Go Back to Where You Came From* – Series 1, Episodes 1, 2 and 3 and *The Response*
- Walker, Lucy, *Waste Land*

NESA has mandated that students must study a related text as part of the common module, and that this should be part of their in-school assessment. However there is NO LONGER a requirement to write about a related text in the HSC examination itself.

WHAT DOES NESA REQUIRE FOR THE COMMON MODULE?

The NESA documentation of the Common Module: Texts and Human Experiences states that students:

- deepen their understanding of how texts represent individual and collective human experiences;

- examine how texts represent human qualities and emotions associated with, or arising from, these experiences;

- appreciate, explore, interpret, analyse and evaluate the ways language is used to shape these representations in a range of texts in a variety of forms, modes and media;

- explore how texts may give insight into the anomalies, paradoxes and inconsistencies in human behaviour and motivations, inviting the responder to see the world differently, to challenge assumptions, ignite new ideas or reflect personally;

- may also consider the role of storytelling throughout time to express and reflect particular lives and cultures;

- by responding to a range of texts, further develop skills and confidence using various literary devices, language concepts, modes and media to formulate a considered response to texts;

- study one prescribed text and a range of short texts that provide rich opportunities to further explore representations of human experiences illuminated in texts;

- make increasingly informed judgements about how aspects of these texts, for example, context, purpose, structure, stylistic and grammatical features, and form shape meaning;

- select one related text and draw from personal experience to make connections between themselves, the world of the text and their wider world;

- by responding and composing throughout the module, further develop a repertoire of skills in comprehending, interpreting and analysing complex texts;

- examine how different modes and media use visual, verbal and/or digital language elements;

- communicate ideas using figurative language to express universal themes and evaluative language to make informed judgements about texts;

- further develop skills in using metalanguage, correct grammar and syntax to analyse language and express a personal perspective about a text

If this is what is required by NESA, we need to examine the concept of human experience carefully so we can adequately respond in these ways. I would recommend that you read the complete document which is on the NESA web site and can be downloaded in Word or Adobe. Understanding this document is an important step in handling the textual material within the guidelines required — remember you are reading for a purpose and should make notes and highlight ideas as you read so that you can develop these ideas later.

UNDERSTANDING THE COMMON MODULE

What are Human Experiences?

The concept of Human Experiences is at the heart of the Common Module.

Human Experiences are experiences of individuals or a group of people (eg a family, society, or nation) in life. There are a very wide range of human experiences which include but go beyond this list:

- feelings or reactions (momentary or long term): love, hate, anger, joy, fear, disgust
- key milestones or stages: birth, childhood, adulthood, marriage, divorce, death
- culture, belonging and identity
- conformity and rebellion
- innocence and guilt, justice
- freedom and repression
- education, vocation, work, sport, leisure
- attraction to a person, idea, group or cause
- opposition to an idea, cause, political system
- religious faith or belief
- extreme events such as an earthquake, avalanche, tsunami
- regular events such as walking, eating, singing, dancing, discussing ideas.

The word *experience* seems innately connected to the human condition and it is something we have each day whether a mundane experience that is repetitive, or something new and dramatic which offers challenges and rewards. Experiences can vary greatly in their impact on individuals, groups and countries. One example might be a war that is a negative experience for a whole population while we may experience the wonder of medicine with a new vaccine for a deadly disease that saves millions of people. We need to note that the module asks for 'experiences' ...we are a combination of different experiences and each has a varying impact. One person's problem is another's challenge depending on perspective, skill set, previous experience and ability.

Experiences are widespread and often shared: this is why people tell their stories and these shared experiences form part of our cultural heritage. These experiences often inform, warn and teach across entire cultural groups and many stories are shared across cultures.

DEFINING HUMAN EXPERIENCES

Now let's attempt to define what human experiences are and shape them into a more coherent and easily understood framework so we can begin our investigation at a basic level of understanding before moving into more complex analysis and looking at how the texts illuminate our understanding of the term.

Dictionary.com defines the term **experience** as:

noun

1. a particular instance of personally encountering or undergoing something:

2. the process or fact of personally observing, encountering, or undergoing something:

3. the observing, encountering, or undergoing of things generally as they occur in the course of time:
   to learn from experience; the range of human experience.

4. knowledge or practical wisdom gained from what one has observed, encountered, or undergone, e.g. *a man of experience.*

5. *Philosophy.* the totality of the cognitions given by perception; all that is perceived, understood, and remembered.

verb

(used with object), **experienced, experiencing.**

6. to have experience of; meet with; undergo; feel,
   e.g. *to experience nausea.*

7. to learn by experience.

idiom

8. **experience religion**, to undergo a spiritual conversion by which one gains or regains faith in God.

Obviously there are a number of definitions according to context but all are applicable to our study in some shape or form, as the range of human experience is so vast. The search for 'new experience' has driven much of the development of people, groups cultures and nations over past millennia. New experiences are always met with excitement and often trepidation as to what change they might bring.

Think historically about how people have reacted to change. It can cause great upheavals in society, with violent reactions while other changes brought through various experiences are welcomed and may change how people live and comprehend the world. Experiences affect us emotionally in many cases rather than logically and when we respond emotionally, behaviours become unpredictable. This causes the paradoxes, anomalies and inconsistencies mentioned in the rubric. If we were logical beings the world would be an easier place, but probably more boring.

These definitions all point to the fact that memory is the key to experience. The experience is stored in memory and drawn upon when the circumstances are repeated or closely mimicked so we can deal with them — hopefully better than on the initial experience.

Experiences can come in many ways and the synonyms listed below for experience help us to understand the concept even further. They assist in defining how an experience can arise:

Synonyms

actions
background
contacts
involvement
know-how
maturity
participation
patience
practice
reality
sense
skill
struggle
training

understanding
wisdom
acquaintances
actuality
caution
combat
doings
empiricism
evidence
existences
exposures
familiarity
intimacy
inwardness

judgment
observation
perspicacity
practicality
proofs
savoir-faire
seasonings
sophistication
strife
trials
worldliness
forebearance

http://www.thesaurus.com/browse/experience?s=t

These synonyms show partly the vast array of words that our language has created around this concept, and also shows how important it is in the human psyche. We, as humans, want to experience. Now we will look at some examples of experiences and examine how they can have an impact. It is also important to remember that experiences do not have to be positive. You might experience a huge problem, a bereavement, a car accident, an unwelcome relationship or something totally bizarre that rocks your world. There can be a more opaque side to any experience that may need to be addressed.

The whole aim of this Common Module is to examine the text closely but also relate it to the concept of human experiences and decide how examining it in this way enables us to better understand both the text and the concept of humanity.

It is important that you unpack what each text you study shows you about human experiences and what ideas / themes arise from those experiences. Formulate your own ideas about the text.

Read the NESA Stage 6 document called *English Stage 6: Annotations of selected texts prescribed for the Higher School Certificate 2019–23* (see *www.educationstandards.nsw.edu.au*) for the set text you are studying. This document offers insights into the way each particular text should be examined by outlining key ideas and areas for clarification.

Human experiences and ways of experiencing vary due to individual circumstance and these experiences can change many things about individual lives, communities and the world. When we examine the concept of human experience in relation to a text, we need to examine the assumptions or biases we bring to it as well as how experiencing the text itself may change us and how we view things. The text may challenge and confront how we view the human experience or we may have preconceived ideas that make it more difficult for this to happen.

Students can also think about their own 'personal experience to make connections between themselves, the world of the text and their wider world.' Examining and enjoying any text is an experience in itself but it is what we take away from the text and apply that is the crucial aspect. That is not to say that every text will be enjoyed or offer a human experience that is significant either positively or negatively. Some texts may not personally engage you and that is fine. This is especially so when you begin to look for other related material that links to *Texts and Human Experiences*. We recommend that you find examples of texts that link but also personally appeal to you so that you can relate empathetically with them.

Individual Human Experiences

The idea of personal experiences is a popular and pervasive concept, especially in the literature of many cultures. Recording personal experiences as a means of sharing wisdom or more mundane daily tasks is part of human nature and we record and relate these experiences frequently. Experiences are recorded and relayed in many ways. We tell oral stories in both anecdotal and formal ways, we write, draw, sing and photograph our way into history (or not). Look at the proliferation of social media in this current century as people record their daily, even hourly, experiences for all to see. We record the most trivial details of our lives for likes and followers while the real world passes us by. Human experiences affect us on a daily basis and some experiences influence our lives and the way we live them.

Individuals seek out experiences in a variety of ways. Some seek more and more extreme experiences to test themselves against the world. Others limit their experiences. A lot of people prefer the familiar and don't actively seek new experiences. Individuals, it must be remembered, also see experiences in different ways and the same experience may have a very different impact on individuals. The one thing we can be certain about is that experiences are part of humanity and even the most limited of us have them. Many of these experiences also come from interaction with others and as noted we also like to share these experiences.

Experiences are what define us in many ways and are what makes us human.

We are going to look at four specific ways that experiences can influence us as people over the next few pages. These are physical, psychological, emotional and intellectual experiences and many experiences are a combination of these.

Physical Experience

The concept of a physical experience is tied into the human experience and part of the collective experience as well. Individuals seek physical experiences to test themselves against nature and other individuals often as part of trials and rituals, for example being integrated into a community. In modern times individuals have sought to test themselves with extreme sports and explorations into the harshest conditions and even space. Physical experiences can also change the way we see the world and others because of the chemical changes these experiences have on our bodies and mind. Physical experiences are often challenges and part of the experience is overcoming adversity. These physical challenges are often celebrated, as in the case of sports, but can also offer challenges if the experience is a negative one such as an accident or disease. Physical experiences are also often quite public and thus have permeated our societies in both their execution and how they are perceived. These physical experiences, even if experienced vicariously, have become popular across cultures and celebrated. Think of examples for yourself but most competitive sports offer examples.

Bruce Lee extends the concept of the physical experience into all aspects of life and that's what we will look at next in our analysis of human experiences –

'*If you always put limits on everything you do, physical or anything else, it will spread into your work and into your life. There are no limits. There are only plateaus, and you must not stay there, you must go beyond them.*'

Psychological Experience

The idea of a psychological experience is tied into many of the abstract ideas that people experience and can lead to a discussion of what is normal psychology. From the earliest times humans have attempted to alter their psychology through a number of experiences. On a simple level this can be a drug that changes the person's or group's perspective on reality. Examples of this might be alcohol or marijuana but cultural groups also use various substances to share group experiences. This can be seen in Native American cultures with *peyote*. In more modern times prescription drugs that are mood altering have been used to minimise the symptoms of psychiatric illnesses such as depression, and these mood altering drugs are common and legal. Others attempt to alter their psychology by seeing specialists in this area while others act out their condition leading to social and criminal issues. When discussing the human experience, psychology is a key issue and will form a part of most studies of experience. When taken too far this search for a new psychological experience can be harmful eg. an addiction.

Carl Jung, the famous psychologist, comments on the problems of addiction for human experiences, stating clearly that excess can be an issue:

"*Every form of addiction is bad, no matter whether the narcotic be alcohol, morphine or idealism.*"

Emotional Experience

According to the psychologist, Robert Plutchik, there are eight basic emotions:

- **Fear** — feeling afraid.
- **Anger** — feeling angry. A stronger word for anger is rage.
- **Sadness** — feeling sad. Other words are sorrow, grief (a stronger feeling, for example when someone has died) or **depression** (feeling sad for a long time without any external cause). Some people think depression is a different emotion.
- **Joy** — feeling happy. Other words are happiness, gladness.
- **Disgust** — feeling something is wrong or nasty
- **Trust** — a positive emotion; admiration is stronger; **acceptance** is weaker
- **Anticipation** — in the sense of looking forward positively to something which is going to happen. **Expectation** is more neutral; **dread** is more negative.

https://simple.wikipedia.org/wiki/List_of_emotions

Emotions are the strongest drivers of human experience and form lasting aspects of any experience. Think about breaking up with someone you love and the emotions that drive behaviours in this situation. People have all sorts of extreme behaviours under the influence of emotions and these experiences are often the ones recorded and those which influence us most. Think about the role emotions play in our lives and the range of emotions from the list above. Consider how much emotions affect our life experiences, how they influence our decisions which decide our experiences and on a higher level consider how they affect the decisions which may seriously impact our experiences, such as politicians going to war.

Intellectual Experience

The concept of an intellectual experience is linked to decisions and experiences we have based on analysis and logic rather than the emotional choices referred to in the previous section. These intellectual experiences have changed the way we live and how we have seen our world. These experiences have affected the way we as humans have altered our world to suit our needs and lead to all the great advances in human society and thus experiences. Changes in our ideas, beliefs etc. alter the way we interact with the world and often these intellectual changes come at great cost.

Think of the time in Europe when the Church dominated and stopped scientific advances by calling them heresy/witchcraft. Open societies are more open to new ideas and this is what has hastened the pace of intellectual experiences as dominant ideologies fall away. Intellectual advances may not have the excitement that the other types produce but perhaps they have a more lasting impact on people, societies and the world in general. Ideas are powerful experiences and people hold beliefs strongly.

Immanuel Kant stated that:

> *"experience without theory is blind, but theory without experience is mere intellectual play."*

Consider this statement in the light of what we have learnt about human experiences. Are they a combination of many factors or can we isolate experiences into simple forms?

What exactly is a human experience?

The titular question reminds us of the old brainteaser: "If a tree falls in a forest and no one is around to hear it, does it make a sound?"

There are two classic responses to this. The more Platonically-minded would say the tree always makes a sound when it falls in the forest. We don't have to be there to hear it; we can imagine the sound of a tree falling in the forest, based on memory of such an event or on the recording of such an event. We know that sound is just vibrating air, and it's safe to say that air always vibrates in response to a tree falling, or a bear growling, or a cicada singing, whether we are there to hear it or not.

The second answer is a more post-structuralist response: the sound doesn't occur on its own; it needs a human ear to be heard. Therefore, if there is no human in the forest to hear the tree fall, then there is no sound. This automatically implies that "experience" of anything requires the presence of a human being, which means there is no such thing as an experience that *isn't* human.

Animal rights activists – or anyone with a beloved pet – would almost certainly reject this notion because it prioritises humans and relegates all other species to a lower class of being: an attitude that most would agree has gotten the human race into an awful lot of environmental trouble over the last 200 years of industrialisation.

In his article (*What is an Experience?*), my learned colleague Paul Hartley describes experience in its most basic form, as "the perception of something else" and "ultimately information about what we have perceived." But does this make it particularly human? Dogs and cats perceive things. Insects perceive things. You could even say that plants perceive things, such as the direction from which the sun is shining. Perception is the most basic of life's survival tools for all manner of flora and fauna.

In her brief but cogent disquisition on the subject (*What is Human?*), another of my learned colleagues, Nadine Hare, asserts that to be human is a social construct. Hartley builds on that notion by suggesting that culture affects experience when we start to share it, because "the words, associations, and priorities we attach to the shared experience define how we understand the world we live in."

Hare rightly points out that this world is increasingly dominated by consumerism, which has distorted what it means to be human by excluding all of the attributes and qualities that "make people people." Calling us consumers reduces our experiences to mere transactions. It defines human experience within the narrow confines of the purchase funnel and has little interest in anything that isn't a purchase driver.

Perhaps the field of commerce is where the experiential rubber most emphatically meets the road. Unlike mere perception, commerce is a uniquely human experience. It has mediated, automated, and dominated the human agenda to the point where we are defined by what we buy and little else. Commerce has invaded the non-profit spheres of government, health, and education, imposing its own priorities and principles on these institutions in the expectation that they will behave more like businesses. And even though business still strives to appeal to the so-called masses, it prioritises the pursuit of individual wealth, and in so doing, not only inhibits the desire for shared experience but unravels the social fabric historically woven by the democratic tradition.

As if in response, that social fabric is being re-woven by our networks. As Hare asserts, "humans both produce technology and are produced through technology." Experience is shared more now than it ever has been because the experiential platform – i.e., that very human invention called the internet – is in place to facilitate it like never before, and on a global scale.

This sharing capability reintroduces all of those things that "make people people" back into the conversation – whether commercial or political. What "makes people people" is messy, unpredictable, emotional, and complex. Most of what makes us human has no place in the experiential confines of the purchase funnel, and defies any of our attempts to place it there.

The challenge for us as a species is to embrace this new capacity for sharing to keep the agendas of our hegemonic institutions – whether commercial or political – from defining what makes an experience human. A post-consumer business strategy might be one that, as Hare hopes, will "expand our view of people to include the complex and dynamic social, cultural, gendered, spiritual and racialised beings that they are." Maybe then will our shared human experience truly become, as Hartley asserts, the glue that holds us all together as human beings.

Will Novosedlik
MISC magazine

https://miscmagazine.com/what-is-a-human-experience/

This article appeared in the September 2014 edition of MISC magazine. Can you relate to what the article says about human experiences? Do human experiences depend on perception? Does the experience of anything require the presence of a human as experiencer (para 3)? Can the ideas of experience be extended to include perception by plants or animals? Hartley's idea is that "shared human experience" is "the glue that holds us all together as human beings". Is this an oversimplification?

The Impact of Human Experiences

Human experiences have impacts on many levels. On an individual level, we can have changes in our assumptions about the world and people around us; we can ingest new ideas and have these open new vistas of productivity and performance. We can also reflect and build on these experiences to ensure that they are even more meaningful to our lives. Behaviours towards others and the way we respond to the world can manifest themselves in new and different responses. An example might be that through adverse experiences we can build resilience so that the next negative experience isn't as traumatic and we accept it for what it is. Experiences also teach us new behaviours on a very physical level — if you burn yourself once on a flame you learn not to do it again (hopefully).

The impact of human experiences can also be shared in groups and societies. Firstly, let's examine some group dynamics that can be affected by human experiences. Groups share experiences and adapt and develop behaviours that impact on the group as a whole. Think about the notorious 'bonding' sessions sporting teams have that unite them in a common goal. Think about the behaviours of various gangs in our society. We see plenty of examples of this on American television where gangs based on ethnicity and social groupings form specific sets of behaviours that impact on how they interact with each other and the world. These groupings carry assumptions about how they see the world and respond to it. For example, they may have generally negative reactions to law enforcement and this is ingrained into their codes of behaviour. They are suspicious of the world and the people in it — dividing them up into threats, the law and victims. These behaviours are often reinforced by group experiences such as the initiation rituals which are integral to membership.

Often the impact of these behaviours is to perpetuate stereotypes that then categorise the individuals within these groups. The graphic I have included here shows a stereotypical gang member with the suspicious gaze, ubiquitous hoody and scruffy look. These stereotypes reject new ideas and maintain assumptions about the world, often to the detriment of their members. The experiences they have reinforce their own stereotypical way of viewing anything outside the safety of the group and the cycle continues. Of course, other groups have more positive impacts and see the world as a  very different place and their experiences are designed to be positive interactions. Think about groups such as Rotary who are constructive in the community. Other groups have specialty interests such as Animal Welfare, Surf Lifesaving and charities.

Normal social interactions impact groups and individuals, but it takes a major event to alter the behaviours of whole societies, especially so in the modern world where societies are large in scale. Earlier in human history smaller experiences could alter the behaviour of societies as they were insignificant in size compared to modern ones. We often fail to remember that many of these ancient societies' behaviours were impacted by superstition, religions and cultural habituation. The modern society as we know it is only a recent phenomenon. Just a few hundred years ago with church rule people were forced to think in a specific

way and punished for not adhering to a theological culture. Think of the Spanish Inquisition, the imprisonment of Galileo and other such restrictions on freedom of thought; scientific breakthroughs were hidden or declared witchcraft. Even recently the world has seen societies kept repressed by failed ideologies. The brutality of such regimes has left deep scars on the social psyche of nations as they try to recover. This has had an impact on the human experiences of whole populations, and societies respond accordingly.

One example might be at the conclusion of the Communist regime in East Germany when the Berlin Wall was destroyed as a visual symbol of the new-found freedom of a whole population of people who had been repressed for decades by a brutal and ever-present regime. Many citizens who had grown up in this system, where you could 'disappear' without trial or real evidence, found the idea that you could express yourself incredible. Many of the

East Germans couldn't believe that this freedom was real and that the Stasi (the secret police) were gone.

Other experiences can affect societies in extreme ways. Think about wars and the impact they have on civilian populations.

Climatic events such as earthquakes change the way that people behave and respond to situations. Catastrophic flooding occurred in the US city of New Orleans in 2005. The US President's response to help was not immediate and the national administration was severely criticised for lack of effective action.

Societies also respond to perceived problems such as pollution. In 1989 the oil tanker Exxon Valdez ran aground in Prince William Sound, Alaska with disastrous results. The effects of this event are still being experienced thirty years later.

Societies can be divided, as we saw with the election of Donald Trump in the United States of America and the reaction of the Political Left.

The impact of human experiences on societies can be quite dramatic, as we have seen, while other experiences (such as an election) can go by without a murmur from societies, no matter who wins. As a last thought before we move on you should also consider the impact of the media on societies in the modern world, and how they influence individuals, societies and the development of ideas.

Problems With Human Behaviour

So far, we have discussed the impact of human experiences on behaviour. Now we can begin to develop some more complex judgements and understandings about the impact of those experiences on human behaviours. In simplistic terms it could be assessed as:

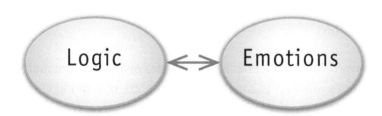

These two opposites on the continuum certainly shape the manner in which we see incidents and how they affect the experience. For instance, if someone you love has no interest in you, it creates a very different reaction to someone you don't care about having no interest in you. It is generally agreed that humans respond more strongly with emotion than they do with logic. Often, it is only through time and reflection that we can understand how an experience has changed and/or altered the manner in which we see a situation or individual.

The Role of Storytelling in Human Experiences

Storytelling has been part of the human experience since 'people' began communicating and it is a method used to convey information and experience as well as be entertaining. Earliest myths were all oral and then people began to write down stories so they weren't lost in time. From this, various theories have developed around storytelling and one is the 'monomyth', which is a template across cultures for storytelling. Let's have a look at this below.

'In narratology and comparative mythology, the monomyth, or the hero's journey, is the common template of a broad category of tales that involve a hero who goes on an adventure, and in a decisive crisis wins a victory, and then comes home changed or transformed.

The concept was introduced in *The Hero with a Thousand Faces* (1949) by Joseph Campbell, who described the basic narrative pattern as follows:

> "A hero ventures forth from the world of common day into a region of supernatural wonder: fabulous forces are there encountered and a decisive victory is won: the hero comes back from this mysterious adventure with the power to bestow boons on his fellow man."

Campbell and other scholars, such as Erich Neumann, describe narratives of Gautama Buddha, Moses, and Christ in terms of the monomyth. Critics argue that the concept is too broad or general to be of much use in comparative mythology. Others say that the hero's journey is only a part of the monomyth; the other part is a sort of different form, or colour, of the hero's journey.

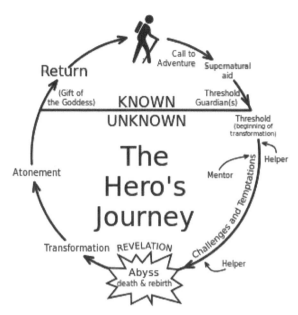

https://en.wikipedia.org/wiki/Hero%27s_journey

Storytelling in History and its Purpose in Human Experience

Storytelling in oral form was accompanied by some theatrics to make the stories as entertaining as possible. Many of the early narratives were based upon religious ceremonies and stories of the creation of the earth and people(s). As time moved on, these stories were accompanied by dance, music and/or theatre and often were part of lengthy rituals, often taking days. These stories were designed to bring meaning to people's lives by explaining their own existence and the purpose/meaning of life in a time when life expectancy was short and entertainment was scarce. Of course stories were also recorded as these experiences were significant to all people and these stories run across all cultures. Before writing, stories were recorded in pictures such as cave art, in tattoo designs on skin and in designs such as rock piles and the giant carved heads of Easter Island.

Writing changed the manner in which stories were told and many of the old oral traditions were lost, barely being kept alive by specialists. Stories began to travel across cultural and national boundaries on whatever surface could be created. Papyrus, bones, pottery, skins, paper and in more modern times film, video and digital storage have changed, over time, the way in which stories of human experience have been told and shared. Content evolved from myth, fable and legend to history, personal narratives and commentary. Modern narrative form often has an educational or didactic element and can drift into propaganda. Stories of self-revelation can be instructive and give audiences the opportunity to apply learning to individual lives, whereas historically narrative was used in this way for societies and groups as a whole. In recent times narratives have become interactive and audiences can choose how the narrative unfolds.

Whatever form the story takes we all have a seemingly innate need for narratives to make sense of our lives. They either confirm our world view or alter our world view depending on the experience they convey and the experiences that we bring to the narrative. We need to remember that narratives are important to human experience and have been significant since the beginning of time.

The Text as an Experience

The concept of the text as an experience is one area to consider as we look at *Texts and Human Experiences*. Reading or viewing the text is an experience in itself and when we do this we bring our own history (experiences) to the text and this helps shape our understanding.

Think about the personal perspective that you bring to a text. What are some of your experiences that might influence how you read a particular text? Some texts, especially personal narratives of trial and tribulation or loss, can be confronting to some audiences and bring back strong opinions or emotions. Many texts attempt to do this as they convey a particular point of view about the world.

Does what you bring to the text affect what you learn from that text? We also need to delve into how the narrative experience is conveyed and how this in turn impacts upon the manner in which the story is received by audiences across different cultures. For example, Western films where heroes fight Islamic terrorism may well be viewed very differently by audiences in Western democracies and Islamic countries. Even seemingly innocuous narratives like the movie 'The Red Pill' which is about men's rights and created by a woman, has caused a polarisation of views wherever it has been shown. Strong personal experiences and viewpoints certainly bring their own understandings to texts.

Questions for Texts and Human Experiences

- Define the module in your own words.
- How are people connected by shared experiences?
- How might physical experience(s) change the way you respond to the world?
- How do you think a person's context and prior experiences shape how they perceive the world?
- Are experiences unique or do prior experiences have an impact on a current experience and way of seeing life?
- What is positive about human experiences?
- Discuss what is negative about human experiences.
- To what extent does experience shape the way we see other people and / or groups?
- Is an individual's culture part of their experience or is it something else?
- Is it possible not to have any meaningful experiences at all?
- Why do people tell stories?
- What do you think you might learn from a narrative?

STUDYING A FICTION TEXT

The medium of any text is very important. If a text is a novel this must not be forgotten. Novels are *read*. This means you should refer to the "reader" but the "responder" can also be used when you are referring to the audience of the text.

The marker will want to know you are aware of the text as a novel and that you have considered its effect as a written text.

Remembering a fiction text is a written text also means when you are exploring *how* the composer represents his/her ideas you MUST discuss language techniques. This applies to any response you do using a novel, irrespective of the form the response is required to be in.

Language techniques are all the devices the author uses to represent his or her ideas. They are the elements of a fiction that are manipulated by authors to make any novel represent its ideas effectively! You might also see them referred to as stylistic devices or narrative techniques.

Every fiction uses language techniques differently. Some authors have their own favourite techniques that they are known for. Others use a variety to make their text achieve its purpose.

Some common language techniques are shown on the diagram that follows.

LANGUAGE TECHNIQUES

Setting – *where does the action take place? Why? Does the setting have symbolic meaning?*

Main Character portrayal/development: *How does the character develop? What is the reader to learn from this?*

Minor Charact⸱ use: *How does author use the minor characte⸱ represent idea⸱ about themes ⸱ major characte⸱*

Narrative Person: *what is the effect this has on the narrative and the reader's response to it?*

LANGUAGE TECHNIQUES

Humour

Symbols and motifs: *how is repetition of image/idea used to maximise the novel's effect?*

Images: *similes, metaphor⸱ personifica⸱*

Dialogue: *not jus⸱ what is said but how is important to idea representation*

Tone: *not just of character comments but also of the narration*

Conflict: *the action, Man vs man, Man vs nature, and/or Man vs himself*

Aural techniques: *Alliteration, assonance and onomatopoeia, rhythm*

THE AUTHOR

'An imaginative and intricate novel inspired by the horrors of World War II and written in short, elegant chapters that explore human nature and the contradictory power of technology.'

http://www.pulitzer.org/winners/anthony-doerr

Doerr's career is summed up in the Wikipedia entry:

> 'Doerr's first published book was a collection of short stories called *The Shell Collector* (2002). Many of the stories take place in Africa and New Zealand, where he has worked and lived. He wrote another book of short stories called *Memory Wall* (2010). His first novel, *About Grace*, was released in 2004. Doerr then wrote a memoir, *Four Seasons in Rome*, which was published in 2007.

> Doerr's second novel, *All the Light We Cannot See*, set in occupied France during World War II, was published in 2014. It received significant critical acclaim and was a finalist for the National Book Award for Fiction.[3] The book was a *New York Times* bestseller and was named by the newspaper as a notable book of 2014.[4] It won the Pulitzer Prize for Fiction in 2015. It was runner-up for the 2015 Dayton Literary Peace Prize for Fiction [5] and won the 2015 Ohioana Library Association Book Award for Fiction.[6]

> Doerr also writes a column on science books for the *Boston Globe* and is a contributor to *The Morning News*, an online magazine.

> From 2007 to 2010, he was the writer-in-residence for the state of Idaho.'

https://en.wikipedia.org/wiki/Anthony_Doerr

The author's webpage can be found at:

http://www.anthonydoerr.com/

If you click on the novel page there is a video of Doerr discussing the novel and its context. More on this next.

PUTTING THE NOVEL IN CONTEXT

Background to World War Two

Considered primarily as a European war because it began when Germany; led by Adolf Hitler, attacked all of Europe. Beginning in Czechoslovakia and moving on to Poland, Norway, Denmark, Belgium and Holland in succession the Germans controlled most of Europe. Soon the world was involved in its most destructive, violent and widespread war in its history. There is a vast amount of information on this war and just remember not to go too far. It's the novel we are interested in!

- *https://en.wikipedia.org/wiki/World_War_II*
- *http://www.historynet.com/world-war-ii*
- *http://world-war-2.info/summary/*
- *http://www.bbc.co.uk/history/worldwars/wwtwo/ww2_summary_01.shtml*

Two videos for those that don't read!

- *https://www.youtube.com/watch?v=wvDFsxjaPaE*
- *https://www.youtube.com/watch?v=HUqy-OQvVtI*

PLOT OUTLINE

Her father is the locksmith and the Natural History Museum in Paris

Marie-Laure is going blind

Werner and Jutta grow up in the orphanage in Germany

The war comes and the Sea of Flames has to be hidden

Werner is sent to a special school because he's smart

The LeBlancs are evacuated from Paris and go to Saint-Malo and Uncle Etienne

Werner's friend Frederick is brain-damaged from a school beating

Saint-Malo becomes occupied by the Germans

Marie-Laure's father is arrested. He has hidden the gem with his daughter

Von Rummel is searching for the gem and is relentless

Preparations are made around the house as the fire comes nearer

As the war turns Werner is sent to the front. Later he ends up in Saint-Malo

Marie-Laure and Etienne continue to work for the resistance

Marie-Laure is still broadcasting. She has little hope.

Etienne is arrested and Von Rummel is in the house searching.

Werner kills Von Rummel and frees Marie-Laure. He is then captured and is killed by a mine

Marie-Laure and Etienne survive and thrive. She has a child and a career. She and Jutta meet.

PLOT SUMMARY

The plot summary that follows contains the salient points for each episode to clarify the narrative but this novel is so good you should read it!

ZERO — 7 AUGUST 1944

Leaflets – the inhabitants of Saint-Malo are warned to leave as the bombers are coming. The war is coming to a conclusion.

Bombers – are heading to France to bomb the German positions in the town.

The Girl – our protagonist, Mari-Laure LeBlanc feels the scale model of the town her father has crafted for her. It is wartime and her great-uncle Etienne hasn't yet returned. She can hear the bombers coming and finds a sheet of paper caught in the window sill.

The Boy – in another part of Saint-Malo Werner Pfennig wakes to the sound of the bombers in the L'hotel des Abeilles (Hotel of Bees) which has fallen into disrepair during the war. On the top floor the anti-aircraft gun fires as Werner heads to the cellar.

Saint-Malo – what's left of the townspeople head to the shelters. Its two months after D-day but the town is one of the last German strongholds on the Breton coast. It has been a siege point for three thousand years and now it waits...

Number 4 rue Vauborel – Marie-Laure stands 'smelling a leaflet she cannot read' knowing she should be heading down to the cellar. She is in the 'tall, derelict bird's nest of a house' owned by Etienne. She takes a miniature house her father crafted and in it is hidden a stone, 'the shape of a teardrop'.

Cellar – Werner is in the cellar playing with his radio with his friend Volkheimer and the engineer Bernd. Werner has forgotten his water but is told they will be safe here. He thinks back to his childhood and hears the radio voices of his childhood.

Bombs Away – The bombers drop their loads, a 'demonic horde' and 72,000lb of explosives rock the town. In Werner's cellar the light 'winks out' as Marie-Laure hides under her bed.

Questions for Zero — August 1944

1. Discuss the narrative technique(s) in this section. How does Doerr engage the audience? What impression have you of the novel from this initial section?

2. Why is the war a good setting? What does such a large landscape of events allow the author to do?

3. What is the 'Sea of Flames? Discuss why Doerr tells us of the story behind the stone.

4. Describe Saint-Malo in your own words.

5. What do you think is going to happen? What human experiences have we encountered to date?

ONE — 1934

Museum National d'Histoire Naturelle – Marie-Laure is six and has 'rapidly deteriorating eyesight' but she is on a tour of the museum where her father is locksmith. The children hear a story about the 'Sea of Flames', a stone from Borneo that carries a curse. The stone's keeper is eternal but those around them die. The stone is hidden in the museum. Marie-Laure asks why it is not thrown into the sea but the warder suggests it is too valuable. One month after this 'she is blind'.

Zollverein – Werner and his little sister, Jutta, are orphans in this coal-mining town and times are hard. Werner is small but exceedingly bright and questioning. They play around town and once visit 'Pit Nine' where their father died.

Key Pound – Marie-Laure's cataracts are permanent and she initially struggles but begins to form patterns in her mind. Her father is in charge of the keys, of which there are many. She learns Braille and is educated by the men of the museum who have the treasures of the world at their fingertips. Her father tells her 'he will never leave her, not in a million years'.

Radio – Werner learns he is clever at electronics and builds a radio which picks up music 'like a miracle'.

Take Us Home – Marie-Laure's father creates 'wooden puzzle boxes' for her birthdays and he begins to teach her how to find her way home. She cannot do it.

Something Rising – Werner experiments with his 'radio receiver' while the other children play. He begins to scavenge parts and the orphanage kids can now listen for an hour. Things are getting better in Germany and nationalistic plays are performed on the radio.

Light – Marie-Laure is finally, in the winter of her eighth year, able to find her way home.

Our Flag Flutters Before Us – Hitler Youth is popular in Zollverein and now the orphan's carer Frau Elena speaks less French. Werner learns all boys will be miners at fifteen. The radio continues to 'chatter' nationalism.

Around the World in Eighty Days – Marie-Laure begins to draw maps in her head and she can find her way around. Her imagination supplies the colour to her touch. She cannot remember her mother and sometimes still becomes lost in the museum but is always returned to her father in the 'key pound'. Her father gives her the Jules Verne book for her birthday and she begins to fall in love with the adventures of Phineas Fogg.

The Professor – Werner and Jutta secretly listen to the radio at night and stumble across a Frenchman with a 'velvet' voice talking about science and Werner is riveted.

Sea of Flames – the museum is going to display the stone and Marie-Laure's father begins to construct a secret display box. Marie-Laure is only concerned about the curse and her father's proximity to the stone.

Open Your Eyes – Werner and Jutta love listening to the Frenchman and they mimic his experiments. Werner notices the sound quality is declining in the broadcasts but they do make Werner realise there is a larger world.

Fade – Marie-Laure's thoughts about the Sea of Flames recedes as time passes to her eleventh birthday when she receives the Braille *Twenty Thousand Leagues Under the Sea*. She spends all day reading.

The Principles of Mechanics – The orphanage is visited by a vice minister and the children are very nervous. Werner has *The Principles of Mechanics* in his lap; an old book he found which he has been allowed keep. He is trying to understand it and the vice minister takes it and tells the boys they are all going down the mines.

Rumors – Rumors suggest the Germans are coming to Paris but her father thinks 'everyone remembers the last war, and no one is mad enough to go through that again'. Later in the year Marie-Laure thinks she can 'smell gasoline under the wind'.

Bigger Faster Brighter – State Youth is now mandatory and Werner is exhausted as he stays up late listening to his radio or doing math. He has become good at repairs and begins to fix people's equipment. He occasionally gets food or money for his work. Jutte tells of a half-Jew who is ostracised as the Hitler Youth begin to become dominant.

Mark of the Beast – Marie-Laure is harassed by some local boys about the horrors of the Germans and she also hears the gossip of the office girls. She begins to have nightmares.

Next we read a letter from Jutta to the Professor which tells how Germany is changing. Jews are persecuted and the poor are vulnerable. It is illegal to listen to foreign broadcasts.

Good Evening. Or *Heil* Hitler if You Prefer – Werner is now fourteen and in 1940 no one laughs at the Hitler Youth anymore. The children still listen to the radio at the orphanage but the Frenchman no longer broadcasts. Werner thinks of the German war machine and how everyone now says '*heil* Hitler'.

Bye-bye, Blind Girl – Now the museum is being cleared as the Germans are coming. Things begin to change; radio stations disappear, the Director is leaving, sandbags appear and Marie-Laure wonders what will happen.

Making Socks – Jutta thinks what is happening in Germany is 'dangerous' and tells Werner the Germans are bombing Paris.

Flight – Across Paris people pack to leave and Marie-Laure is taken by her father to the train station where they hope to catch one.

Herr Seidler – A lance corporal comes to collect Werner to fix a radio. They arrive at the 'largest house' where Rudolf Seidler and Frau Seidler greet them. The man has a 'massive American Philco' that needs repairs. It is the best radio Werner has ever seen and he manages to fix it 'just by thinking' says Frau Seidler. Werner is given huge slices of creamy cake and Seidler suggests Werner might be better at a school for 'Exceptional boys'. He gives Werner money and tells him he'll write a letter of recommendation. Back at the orphanage he looks around and wants this new world. He goes out into the alley and destroys his shortwave radio.

Exodus – The train never arrives and Marie-Laure and her father have to walk to Evreux where a friend of the museum will take them in. when Marie-Laure is asleep her father opens his bag and looks at the blue stone he carries. There are four – three copies and he doesn't know if this one is real.

Questions for One — 1934

1. How has the war changed things for both Marie-Laure and Werner?

2. Why is Marie-Laure's father carrying the stone?

3. What is an 'exodus'?

4. Discuss why there might be gossip and rumor surrounding the invading Germans. Why might Marie-Laure be especially upset?

5. How have the experiences of either Marie-Laure *or* Werner shaped them to date?

TWO — 8 AUGUST 1944

Saint-Malo – the town is being destroyed by the bombs and a firestorm erupts.

Number 4 rue Vauborel – Marie-Laure and the house survive and she thinks

Hotel of Bees – Werner is now trapped in the cellar and shouts into the dark 'Have we died?'

Down Six Flights – Marie-Laure thinks she needs to be lower than the sixth floor and works her way down, finally going into the cellar and pulling the trapdoor shut.

Trapped – Volkheimer turns his field light on and they find Bernd badly injured. The light only tells them they are trapped and there is *'no other way out'*.

Questions for Two — 8 August 1944

1.   Discuss the impact of the bombing on the town.

2.   Why does Marie-Laure move?

3.   Describe Werner's reaction to being trapped.

4.   Did you expect these events to happen?

5.   How are the experiences they are having more extreme?

THREE — JUNE 1940

Chateau – Marie-Laure and her father make for Evreux but the chateau is on fire and is being looted. The owner, Monsieur Giannot has already left for London. Her father knows they have to keep going as 'Someone' might be after them for what he carries. He picks the padlock on a barn and they find food in the farm garden. He decides they will go to 'crazy' Uncle Etienne in Saint-Malo.

Entrance Exam- Werner has to go to Essen and the exams last eight days. They are tested and train and it is Werner's first time away from Zollverein. Exams are also about race and Werner shows his courage by jumping into the flag while others fail.

Brittany- Marie-Laure and her father get a lift in a furniture truck until it runs out of fuel. They walk to the ocean and finally to their uncle's house.

Madame Manec - The pair are invited in and Madame tells them 'the town is stuffed' and then proceeds to feed them. Marie-Laure falls asleep.

You Have Been Called - Werner is back at the orphanage and five days later a letter arrives which says *'You have been called'*. Everything is paid for and everyone is excited for him except Jutta.

Occuper – Marie-Laure awakes in a bed and Madame tells her about Uncle Etienne and how the last war changed him. He is odd and reclusive yet Marie-Laure is still excited to be near the ocean. Many people are displaced and the Germans are occupying France. Marie-Laure is worried about their little apartment in Paris.

Don't Tell Lies – Werner can't concentrate on anything and he cannot find a way to explain his choice to an unhappy Jutta, who knows of the 'atrocities' the Germans have committed via the radio. He makes excuses but she says, 'Lie to yourself, Werner, but don't lie to me'.

Etienne – on the fifth day Marie-Laure follows a trail of shells to her uncle's room and she gets a tour of his 'big room'. In the town Marie-Laure's father sees the Germans come in.

Jungmänner – Werner's school is a castle and the rules are tight. It is all about 'country' and 'nation'. Werner makes friends with Frederick a pale, thin boy. Lessons are on various subjects including race and physical fitness. Werner has a 'hunger to belong' and the boys have a nationalistic fervour.

Vienna – Sergeant Major Reinhold von Rumpel is a gemmologist who ran a small business before the war but now values 'confiscated' items and sends them back to the Fuhrer. He reads about the 'Sea of Flames' and decides it is this he needs to find.

The Boches – The Germans are everywhere and Marie-Laure is unable to go out so she explores the house. Madame Manec's friends fuss over the girl.

Hauptmann – Dr Hauptmann is the instructor of technical sciences and Werner impresses him immediately.

Flying Couch – The Germans collect all firearms as her father continues to build her a model of the town. Marie-Laure listens to Etienne read Darwin's *The Voyage of the Beagle* and in the evening they play 'Flying Couch' and travel all over the world.

The Sum of Angles – Werner is called to Dr Hauptmann's office and he fives the boy some trigonometry to do. Werner is assigned to work with him and the huge boy Volkheimer is to 'keep an eye out for him'. Frederick wants to talk about an owl back in the barracks but is told to be silent by the other boys.

The Professor – Etienne explains to Marie-Laure why he never leaves the house. They go to the garret and he tells her of his dead brother who had a 'dream' voice. They made science recordings together before the war. Etienne tells how his brother died and how he transmitted the recordings hoping some children would hear them. He also hoped his brother would hear but he never answered back.

Werner's letters to his sister are slightly censored but he tells her about the school and Frederick.

Perfumer – Claude Levitte (Big Claude) is the town perfumer who begins to make money from the misery of the war. Claude admires the Germans. He sees Marie-Laure's father measuring the street for his daughter's model and decides to report him to the Germans. He thinks it's a good opportunity.

Time of the Ostriches – German occupation has brought many rules and austerity and Marie-Laure is unhappy they cannot return to Paris. Many call it the time of the ostriches because people keep their heads in the sand.

Weakest – Bastian the officer in charge of field exercises and one day he pulls the 'weakest member' of the group, Ernst to run. He has a ten second head start on the other forty-nine boys. If he is caught who knows what will happen but he makes it by a split second to the commandant.

Mandatory Surrender – The Germans now decree all radios have to be surrendered. It is a major job as Etienne has so many and it takes Marie-Laure's father several trips. Etienne doesn't appear.

Museum – Rumpel goes to the museum and after a tour asks to see the things they have not shown him. They claim there is nothing but he waits, particularly wanting to see the Sea of Flames. Rumple vaguely threatens their children before they succumb and take him to the gem.

The Wardrobe – Etienne finally learns of the removal of his radios. He and Marie-Laure hide the radio in the attic by covering the door with a huge wardrobe.

Blackbirds – Werner works nights with Hauptmann and Werner notices that the doctor and Volkheimer are full of contradictions as people. His friend Frederick is focused on birds and hates his fellow cadets for shooting them.

Daniel le Blanc gets a telegram to return to Paris at the end of the month with the words 'TRAVEL SECURELY' added.

Bath – Marie-Laure's father completes the model of Saint-Malo but despite this he feels 'ragged' thinking about the stone and the misfortune it brings. He has tried to get rid of it but he can't. At the train station he sees the perfumer and returns home to tell Marie-Laure he is leaving. He is proud of her and how he has raised her. He tells her as she bathes that he will be gone ten days and no more.

Weakest (#2) – This time Frederick is picked as the weakest and is soon caught. Rodel beats Frederick with a hose and Werner does nothing but thinks Frederick is stronger than him in every way. Frederick will not admit he is the weakest and runs back bloody.

The Arrest of the Locksmith – Marie-Laure's father is taken prisoner on the train and questioned before being sent to Germany. He thinks only of Marie-Laure.

Questions for Three — June 1940

1. Discuss the transition of Werner from the orphanage to school. Why do you think Jutta is unhappy?

2. What do we learn about the experiences of Etienne? How have these experiences changed his life?

3. Describe your reaction to the idea of the 'weakest'. What does this exercise show about human nature?

4. Did you think Marie-Laure's father would be arrested?

5. How limiting are the experiences Marie-Laure has because of her blindness? Do you think her inability to see makes her emotional responses different to experiences?

FOUR — AUGUST 1944

The Fort of La Cite – Rumpel knows his cancer is spreading but he looks out and sees Number 4 rue Vauborel is still intact across town. He is waiting for his opportunity to get to the house and find the stone.

Atelier de Reparation – The three men under the rubble survive but with no way out. Werner thinks it is time to make reparations.

Two Cans – Marie-Laure finds two cans of food – 'miracles' – and thinks of her past.

Number 4 rue Vauborel – Rumpel makes it to the house

What They Have – The three trapped men have little food and water, two grenades, a rifle and some light. The radio is gone and Werner is despondent but Volkheimer tells him to think of his sister.

Trip Wire – Marie-Laure decides to eat and has water but as she goes to open the can she hears the trip wire sound and knows someone is in the house.

Questions for Four — August 1944

1. Discuss the significance of von Rumpel being in the town.

2. Analyse Marie-Laure's situation. What would you do in her situation?

3. Describe Werner's response to his situation. Why does Volkheimer try to make him be positive?

4. Think about the different experiences that Doerr has his characters in. Do they need to coalesce?

FIVE — JANUARY 1941

January Recess – Frederick invites Werner to Berlin during the holidays and Werner is amazed, especially at the elevator in Frederick's apartment block. The family have a maid, Fanni, and plenty of money. Frederick shows Werner and amazing book of birds by 'Audubon' but it needs to be hidden because it is American. Frederick's mother comes home and she is pleased to have Werner there. They go out to dine and on return Frederick tells Werner how his parents need him to be at Schulpforte and his life isn't his own.

He is Not Coming Back – Marie-Laure often thinks she hears her father but it's illusory. Etienne learns her father never arrived in Paris but can do nothing and she feels her father is slipping away.

Prisoner – Bastian has Volkheimer tie a 'skeletal' prisoner to a stake in the snow. Bastian makes up a story about the 'barbarian' and how he is 'circling the drain'. Each student is to throw a bucket of water over the man and Frederick alone refuses to do so as the man is already dead. He says emphatically 'I will not'.

Plage du Môle – Marie-Laure's father has been gone for twenty-nine days and Madame Manec takes her down to the beach. On return she brings Etienne some treasures from the sea.

Lapidary – Von Rumpel continues his work but his focus is on the Sea of Flames as the one he found in the museum was a fake. He tracks down Dupont, the man who made the fakes, and has him arrested. Von Rumpel is keen to interrogate him.

Marie-Laure's father sends her an optimistic letter from prison.

Entropy – The prisoner remains tied to the stake for a week frozen until he is eventually taken away. Frederick is always chosen as the weakest and beaten but he refuses to leave. Werner tries to focus on his work and Volkheimer tells him that they do that each year to a prisoner. Frederick is persecuted mercilessly and Werner tries to help him. Hauptmann tells the class the Reich is all about order.

The Rounds – Marie-Laure now goes to the beach every day and collects much. It is the only time she forgets her father. She goes out with Madame on her rounds and begins to know the town and its people including 'Crazy Hubert Bazin'. She uses the model her father made to reinforce her learning. She hopes his letter was true and he has enough to eat.

Nadel im Heuhaufen (Needle in a haystack) – Hauptmann and Werner have to triangulate to find a hidden Volkheimer and they are successful. Werner is ecstatic.

Proposal – Madame Manec and six of her friends decide to do 'smaller things' to get back at the *'Boches'*.

You Have Other Friends – Frederick is bullied mercilessly and tells Werner one night it might be better for Werner if they weren't friends anymore. Werner feels the weight of his past watching him to see what he will do.

Old Ladies Resistance Club – The women plan little annoyances on the Germans including writing *'Free France Now'* on banknotes.

Diagnosis – Von Rumpel now knows there are three copies and he needs a biopsy on his growth.

Weakest (#3) – Werner learns Frederick has been beaten and sent to Leipzig for surgery. He will not be back.

Marie-Laure's father's letter is very positive. He tells her he is well fed and safe.

Grotto – Bazin takes Marie-Laure and Madame down to the sea wall where he unlocks a door to a 'low grotto'. On the way home Bazin gives Marie-Laure the key

Intoxicated – The Germans are winning the war and Werner is fifteen. Frederick has been permanently brain damaged from his beating and Volkheimer has gone to fight the war. To Werner the boys around him seem 'intoxicated' with war fervour. He misses Jutta but her letters are so censored they say little. He is lucky he is important and therefore protected but he wonders about where his life is going.

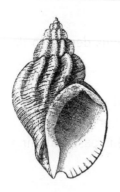

The Blade and The Whelk – At dinner in the Hotel-Dieu Madame Manec makes contact with the resistance and Marie-Laure chooses the pseudonym 'The Whelk' while Madame chooses 'The Blade'.

Jutta's letter arrives slightly censored and with it comes Werner's childhood notebook which makes him homesick.

Alive Before You Die – Madame tries to enlist Etienne to help in her resistance work but he refuses, worried about Marie-Laure.

No Out – It is January 1942 and Werner asks to visit his sister. Hauptmann refuses and Werner knows he is trapped.

The Disappearance of Hubert Bazin – Bazin disappears and the women decide to take a break. People vanish all the time and the rumours are wild.

Everything Poisoned – The school is changing as the war turns; instructors go and are replaced by the elderly and incompetent, the electricity fails, food becomes poor and yet surprisingly all the news is good. Cadets are told when their fathers are killed and it is becoming frequent. The propaganda gets worse. Dr Hauptmann is called to Berlin.

Visitors – Two French policeman come to the house and tell how Marie-Laure's father has been convicted of 'theft and conspiracy' and sent to prison. They don't trust the policeman. They say the museum is searching for him and they ask all about his work, his keys and then they search the house. They find three French flags and Etienne burns them warning Madame not to endanger them.

Werner's letter is heavily censored.

The Frog Cooks – Madame disappears for long periods and there is tension in the house.

Orders – Werner is told he is eighteen despite the fact he is patently younger and is to get instructions as to when he leaves for the front and 'a special technology division of the Wehrmacht'.

Pneumonia – Madame becomes extremely ill.

Papa's letter to Marie-Laure is more realistic but still full of optimism.

Treatments – Von Rumpel has treatment for his cancer.

Heaven – Madame Manec is recovered and she and Marie-Laure resume their walks.

Frederick – Werner visits Frederick but he is basically a vegetable with each eye 'a stagnant pool'.

Relapse – Madame Manec gets sick again and dies.

Questions for Five — January 1941

1. Discuss the negative aspects of Frederick's experience at the school. What is it about him and the way he sees the world that doesn't allow him to fit in?

2. Analyse Von Rumpel's situation. Why is he so focused on the one gem? How does he see the world?

3. Describe Madame Manec's response to the German occupation of her town. Do you think she is sensible in working for the Resistance? Why might someone take risks?

4. Why is Etienne resistant to new experiences and refuses to work with his housekeeper? How do his past experiences impact on his attitude to the present.

SIX — 8 AUGUST 1944

Someone in the House – Marie-Laure knows someone, but not Etienne, is in the house. She is distressed but tries to settle her mind. The footsteps are slow but she recognises the familiarly odd gait of the German Sergeant-major she met at the grotto. She goes up and hides.

The Death of Walter Bernd – Bernd dies entombed after telling the story of his disappointing visit with his father.

Sixth-floor Bedroom – Von Rumpel find's Marie-Laure's room and sees the model town and thinks this is where the stone is hidden.

Making the Radio – Werner gets the radio going but he hears only static.

In the Attic – Marie-Laure sneaks carefully to the attic to open a can of food.

Questions for Six — 8 August 1944

1. Discuss why Marie-Laure is distressed at a visitor in the house. Why might this new experience be unsettling for her?

2. Analyse the story Bernd tells about his father. Why does Doerr include this? Is his death relevant in any way to the narrative?

3. Why does Werner try to make the radio work?

SEVEN — AUGUST 1942

Prisoners – Werner is in the Wehrmacht with two Neumann's and they escort him to the front. On the way they see a prison train with the dead piled up.

The Wardrobe – Etienne leaves his study eventually after Madame Manec's death and he feels better. He creates a secret door in the wardrobe to reach the attic and then he decides to help the Resistance. Marie-Laure is to go to the baker to collect the information and he will broadcast it.

East – Werner arrives in Russia and is given a post without any explanation. He finds the transceiver he designed with Hauptmann and then Volkheimer appears in the back of the truck canopy.

One Ordinary Loaf – Marie-Laure collects the loaf with the information and Etienne says he'll broadcast it at night and does.

Volkheimer – With Bernd they are now a team of five and their mission is to find broadcasts from illegal transceivers. The last technician was hopeless but Werner gets the equipment working. Still he can't find anything.

Fall – Etienne finally 'feels alive' because of the work and now wants to live.

Sunflowers – In the Ukraine Werner finally comes across some static and the do the math and find the enemy. They kill the partisans and burn the house down.

Stones – Von Rumpel is tasked with identifying thousands of jewels from the spoils of war.

Grotto – One day Marie-Laure heads to the beach and goes to the grotto before heading home with the broadcast information.

Hunting – Werner finds a second partisan radio, then more and the team are praised. When they pass a group of prisoners Volkheimer will stop and take the clothes off other giant men. Losing your boots means death but the prisoners always cave-in. the cycle continues and 'Werner does not write to his sister'.

The Messages – Each day Marie-Laure goes to the bakery and at night Etienne reads her the letters from her father. Marie-Laure and Etienne find the letters confusing – they speculate that there is a hidden message that they cannot understand.

Loudenvielle – Von Rumpel awaits a burglar who has robbed the chateau of a donor to the National Museum. The thief has one of the fake gems but he does also take the letters the man has also stolen.

Gray – Marie-Laure's world has turned to gray as Saint-Malo suffers under the Nazis, winter and the smoke from burning green wood.

Fever – Werner is extremely ill with fever yet he still manages to catch illegal transmissions. The Germans are now retreating and Werner wonders about the point of it all.

The Third Stone – Von Rumpel is at the home of another museum worker who fled Paris. The Gestapo crack the safe and inside is another gem, a fake. Von Rumpel thinks he is out of luck as the Germans are losing the war and he is running out of time. He doesn't give up hope and thinks of the puzzle box at the museum.

The Bridge - A German truck is blown up on the bridge and the local people are under great pressure but they keep broadcasting and passing messages. Marie-Laure hopes they are on the side of the 'good guys'.

Rue des Patriarches – Von Rumpel is at the Paris apartment of the Le Blancs. He spies the original model Marie-Laure's father built and realises it is the locksmith who is clever enough to hide the jewel. Von Rumpel then destroys the little house as it may hide the jewel.

White City – Werner and the team are now in Vienna and they head to the Leopoldstadt area to search for illegal radios. They give each other haircuts and in the afternoon Werner watches a little red-haired girl play in the park. Later he thinks he finds an antenna but it a false alarm. Nevertheless Nuemann Two murders the girl who hides in the wardrobe. Werner feels as if he is in 'an engulfing spiral'.

Twenty Thousand Leagues Under the Sea – For her sixteenth birthday Marie-Laure gets both parts one and two of the Braille version of Jules Verne's novel – a gift from her friends in the town.

Telegram – The new commandant in Saint-Malo wants the broadcasts stopped and telegrams Berlin for assistance.

Questions for 7 — August 1942

1. Discuss why the death of the red-haired girl in Vienna affects Werner so much.

2. Describe how Etienne is changing because of his experiences after helping the Resistance.

3. Why is Von Rumpel still hopeful after three setbacks? What do you think of him as a character?

4. How do Marie-Laure's experiences during the war affect her judgement of the stone? Do you think she is realistic in her appraisal of the impact of the stone?

EIGHT — 9 AUGUST 1944

Fort National – The shelling of Saint-Malo 'lulls' and then one stray round kills nine Frenchmen out of three hundred and eighty who are being held against their will in the town.

In the Attic – The bells of St Vincent's have stopped ringing so Marie-Laure has no idea of the time. She is extremely thirsty and thinks of the gem and her father. She can hear von Rumpel downstairs groaning and muttering. She manages to open a can hiding he noise as the shells scream overhead.

The Heads – Werner can't get any reception and the battery is nearly dead. He and Volkheimer wait.

Delirium – Von Rumpel thinks he has taken too much morphine. He thinks the fact that the house is still standing means the gem is there. He means to search it thoroughly.

Water – Marie-Laure hears the German move and the rain begin. She takes the empty can and goes down to her room. She gets water and heads back up to the attic.

The Beams – Volkheimer and Werner both say they wanted to leave where they were born but now...?

The Transmitter – Marie-Laure goes back upstairs, moves the antennae up, takes the microphone and begins to read.

Voice – Now trapped for four days Werner hears the girl reading and is entranced by her final words. He wants to save her as the city is pounded to dust.

Questions for Eight — 9 August 1944

1.   Did you learn anything new about human experiences in this section?

2.   Analyse how Marie-Laure's experiences are often based around the sense of sound.

3.   Why does Werner want to save the girl?

NINE — MAY 1944

Edge of the World – Volkheimer reads Jutta's letter to Werner as they head into France and stop in Epernay. Eventually they reach Saint-Malo and Werner jumps out of the truck and heads to the beach missing the beach mined signs. The commandant tells them of the broadcasts and Volkheimer reassures them the perpetrators will be found.

Numbers – The doctor gives von Rumpel three to four months to live and he gets a call alerting him to Daniel LeBlanc and his time in Saint-Malo.

May – Marie-Laure is told at the bakery that the allies are coming and she goes to the grotto. She hopes her father will be alright.

Hunting (Again) – Werner begins the search in Saint-Malo. He also writes to his sister again.

"Clare de Lune" – Werner picks up the broadcast and hears the music. He decides not to report it.

Antenna – At the Hotel of Bees Werner is concerned about not revealing the transmission but he walks around until he finds the antenna at Number 4.

Big Claude – Von Rumpel thinks Claude is self-important but Claude does reveal that Le Blanc lived across the road at Number 4.

Boulangerie – Werner watches the house and waits to knock at the door but Marie-Laure comes out. He watches her walk to the bakery and as she passes on her return he thinks of 'the pure they were always lecturing about at Schulpforte'.

Grotto – Marie-Laure goes to the bakery, gets the bread and heads to the grotto. On the way she is stopped by a German who questions her about her father. She retreats into the grotto locking the door behind her. 'She is the Whelk. Armored. Impervious.'

Agoraphobia – Etienne is concerned that Marie-Laure is late and begins to hyperventilate. He last left the house twenty-four years ago but that didn't go well. He now steps outside again.

Nothing – Von Rumpel questions her through the gates of the grotto. He wants to know if her father left her anything. She angrily says he 'left me *nothing*'. Her tone convinces him.

Forty Minutes – Etienne goes out and Madame Ruelle helps him out. They run to the grotto and Marie-Laure can only say, 'You came'.

The Girl – Werner thinks of the girl and has so many questions. The two Neumanns are sent to the front and their eyes show 'despair'. Werner decides how to hide his ability to hear the broadcast.

Little House – Etienne is worried about the girl so he braves the outside world and goes to the bakery himself. She thinks again of her father's letter, goes upstairs and finds the gem in the model of Etienne's house.

Numbers – Etienne is given a dangerous job getting gun co-ordinates.

Sea of Flames – Marie-Laure thinks the rock that she holds has caused 'sorrow'. She doesn't tell Etienne and replaces the stone in the house. Etienne goes to get the co-ordinates, breaking curfew, but before he does he tells her 'You are the best thing that has ever come into my life'.

The Arrest of Etienne Le Blanc – Etienne is arrested that night by von Rumpel.

7 August 1944 – Marie-Laure wakes and Etienne has not returned. She fills buckets with water while she can but is disturbed by Big Claude at the door. She refuses to leave the house and he goes away.

Leaflets – Werner is pleased he kept the girl safe. He sees out the window and spies the falling leaflets warning the inhabitants to leave.

Questions for Nine — May 1944

1. Do you feel Marie-Laure is experienced enough to survive without Etienne? Explain your response fully

2. Is it realistic that both Etienne and Werner are obsessed with Marie-Laure?

3. Try and forecast the conclusion of the novel based on your experience of the world and literature.

TEN — 12 AUGUST 1944

Entombed – Werner listens to Marie-Laure's broadcast. He talks to an unresponsive Volkheimer.

Fort National – Etienne tries to get back to Marie-Laure but he is held by the Germans. He dreams of escape and slips back into his past.

Captain Nemo's Last Words – Marie-Laure keeps reading as she hears the German below shout in frustration. She decides to finish the novel and the idea of the whelks strengthens her resolve.

Visitor – Von Rumpel has spent four days in the house and is beginning to doubt the gem is there. A corporal comes and tells him the Germans are retreating and giving up the town. Von Rumpel stays.

Final Sentence – Volkheimer doesn't stir and they have no water. Werner hears Marie-Laure finish the novel. He thinks back into the past as the whole world seems to shake.

Music #1 – Marie-Laure sets the music and the microphone up and it begins as she plans to open her final can of food.

Music #2 – In the cellar Volkheimer hears the music and it stirs him into action. He builds a wall and throws a grenade to try and clear the rubble from the stairwell.

Music #3 – Von Rumpel thinks of his children as he hears the music and then he discerns the voice of a young man above him.

Out – The grenade blows a hole and Volkheimer manages to clear more rubble and they are free. He tells Werner to take the rifle and go to the girl. Werner heads to Number 4 to save her.

Wardrobe – Von Rumpel begins to inspect the wardrobe and then he hears someone enter the house.

Comrades – Werner heads up for the girl and finds a bucket of water which he drinks from. Von Rumpel enters the room and thinks Werner wants the gem. Von Rumpel points his gun at Werner and is then distracted by a noise from above so Werner lunges for his rifle.

The Simultaneity of Instants – Marie-Laure comes down the ladder, Volkheimer eats, Etienne decides if they survive they will go away, Von Rumpel's wife and children go to Mass, Jutta sleeps and finally Werner speaks to Marie-Laure in French asking 'Are you there?'

Are You There? – Werner speaks to Marie-Laure and she comes out.

Second Can – Werner promises to get her out and tells her he listened to the broadcasts as a boy. They share a can of peaches.

Birds of America – She shows Werner around the house and he finds a copy of the book that Frederick had so loved. He takes a page and Marie-Laure asks him if he knew what the other man in the house wanted. Werner assumes it was the radio and they sleep.

Cease – fire – The pair leave the house with Werner helping her negotiate the streets. She takes him on a detour to the grotto and she leaves the house with the gem in the 'ocean'. As they near safety he gives her a 'white flag' and they separate. When they part he opens his hand and finds a key.

Chocolate – Madame Ruelle finds Marie-Laure and they gorge on confiscated chocolate as the Americans free the town. Despite being allowed back days later Etienne and Marie-Laure go to Rennes, book into a hotel and have a long bath each. They plan to go to Paris.

Light – Werner is captured and taken to a holding compound. He can't hold down food and is deaf in one ear. He is sent east and then to Dinan. As he marches he sees no future and becomes so ill he is hospitalised. One night he gets up and heads out across a field in a daze. Ignoring calls to stop he is blown up by a mine set by the Germans.

Questions for Ten — 12 August 1944

1. Analyse why Marie-Laure's transmissions are so important to the narrative. Why might the experiences they arouse cause people to remember and perhaps initiate new experiences?

2. Why does Marie-Laure leave the Sea of Flames floating in the ocean at the grotto?

3. Critique this section of the novel. Does it all come together too easily? Is the escape from the cellar by Volkheimer believable? Think about the connections and shared experiences between people. Is it too coincidental to make the narrative effective? Discuss your response with direct reference to the text.

ELEVEN — 1945

Berlin – Jutta is fifteen and working in a Berlin factory. Things are hard in the factory and they have little of anything. The city is bombed constantly at night. In 'late March' the factory closes and they are moved to cleaning rubble from streets. Then Jutta receives word Werner is dead. By April it is fear of the Russians and they hear horrific stories. When the Russians came in May there are only three soldiers but they rape the women, including Jutta.

Paris – Etienne rents the LeBlanc flat and they search the prisoner lists in vain. Etienne and Marie-Laure spend time at the museum and he tries to maintain her hope. In the Autumn Marie-Laure decides she wants to go to school.

Questions for Eleven — 1945

1. Discuss the episode in Berlin. Why might Doerr include this as an experience for both the reader and Jutta?

2. Does Marie-Laure's life now include hope?

TWELVE — 1974

Volkheimer – Volkheimer is now fifty-one and installing television antenna. He works mostly alone and is haunted by the war. One day he receives a letter which has photos of Werner's bag. Volkheimer thinks of Werner as a boy.

Jutta – Jutta Wette is a maths teacher, married to a 'kind, slow-moving, and balding accountant'. They have one child, Max, who makes paper aeroplanes obsessively. One evening a knock at the door breaks the routine and it is Volkheimer at the door. He asks if her maiden name was 'Pfennig'. Inside they talk about the war and Jutta becomes upset thinking back about Werner and she watches Max and Volkheimer make planes.

Duffel – Werner's duffel waits on the table now that Volkheimer has gone. She waits and tries to distract herself but eventually succumbs to opening it. Inside are a model house, his book from their childhood and a letter 'For Frederick'. She sits and thinks into the night.

Saint-Malo – Jutta and Max head to Saint-Malo and arrive 'around midnight'. They go to the beach, climb the tower of the chateau and explores the relics of the war. At the museum she shows the miniature house to a man who leads her to 'Number four rue Vauborel', the 'LeBlanc house'. She learns of the 'blind girl' and Max works out how to open the house. The man says he has the girl's address in Paris.

Laboratory – Marie-Laure LeBlanc studies molluscs and is very successful. Etienne died at age eighty-two and left her money despite them both travelling extensively. They could never find out exactly what happened to her father except he had been in certain camps and contracted influenza. She still lives in the flat and has a child to one of her two lovers. Helene is nineteen and self-possessed. Marie-Laure still has some issues because of the war but for 'portions of every day, she is happy'. One 'Wednesday evening in July' she gets a visit from a woman with a 'model house'.

Visitor – The woman speaks French from her childhood and the model house is produced. The son is sent to look at beetles with the assistant and Marie-Laure learns that Werner is dead. It is a difficult conversation but Jutta says she wants Marie-Laure to have the house. Marie-Laure says she will mail Max the last remaining recording, the one about the light on the other side of the moon.

Paper Aeroplane – Jutta gets back to the hotel with Max and rings her husband.

The Key – Marie-Laure sits in memories and holds the miniature. She thinks Werner may have used the key but when she opens it the iron key drops into her palm.

Sea of Flowers – The gem is now encrusted with algae, barnacles and snails. It stirs among the pebbles.

Frederick – Frederick lives in Berlin with his mother just drawing spirals on sheets of paper. He gets a letter from Jutte which contains Werner's letter for him. Inside is a folded print of two birds but he 'retains no memories'. They just sit and look 'out at the night'.

Questions for Twelve — 1974

1. Describe briefly what has happened to each of the characters since the conclusion of the war.

2. Discuss Doerr's references to light in this section. How does he use light to draw various concepts together?

THIRTEEN — 2014

Marie is taken by 'her grandson Michel' to the gardens. At the gazebo he plays a computer game and they talk about the Jules Verne book she got for her twelfth birthday. She thinks of the 'electromagnetic waves' that connect people. He takes her back to the apartment and she listens 'until his footsteps fade'.

Questions for Thirteen — 2014

1. How does Doerr think about connections? Base your response on Marie-Laure's thoughts in this section.

2. Did you enjoy the story? Discuss ONE of the experiences in the text that contributed something to your understanding of the world.

SETTING

While the text does range of much of Europe it is basically set in Paris and Saint-Malo in France just prior to and post-World War Two as far as Marie-Laure's narrative is concerned. With the Werner narrative we spend most of the time in Germany but he does go to the Ukraine and Austria before Saint-Malo. We begin in Paris at the apartment near the Natural History Museum. It is here that the LeBlanc's live and Marie-Laure is learning to live without sight. She has a patient father who builds her a model of the

area from which she can learn to find her way around. She also loves exploring the museum but occasionally gets lost. Marie-Laure's human experiences are somewhat defined by her loss of sight and she experiences much through the other senses. An example might be;

> 'She still counts the storm drains: thirty-eight on the walk home from her laboratory. Flowers grow on her tiny wrought-iron balcony, and in summer she can estimate what time of day it is by feeling how wide the petals of the evening primroses have opened. When Helene is out with her friends, and the apartment seems to quiet....' (p512)

Paris in 2014. Photos credit author

In Saint-Malo her world changes and she has the sensory perception to adapt to her new environment,

> 'Marie-Laure listens to the house timbers creak and the gulls cry and the gentle roar breaking against the window. "Are we high in the air, Madame?"' (p126)

Marie is able to survive in her world and thrives back in Paris after the war. She travels with Etienne and makes a career for herself in her laboratory. Saint-Malo is completely destroyed by the bombardment except for a few places like Number 4 rue Vauborel but it is rebuilt. It is Werner who guides her through the rubble to safety because of the connection they have through the broadcasts of her relatives.

Werner has a completely different experience,

> 'Werner Pfennig grows up three hundred miles northeast of Paris in a place called Zollverein: a four-thousand-acre coal-mining complex outside Essen, Germany. It's steel country, anthracite country, a place full of holes. Smokestacks fume and locomotives trundle back and forth on elevated conduits and leafless trees stand atop slag heaps like skeleton hands shoved up from the underworld.' (p24)

Life in the orphanage with his sister, Jutta, is hard and they have care but little else. Werner's talent and engineering from a young age allows him to leave this behind and move to one of 'General Heissmeyer's schools. Best of the best.' It is here that Werner learns the cruelty of the Reich and the opportunities that life offers. The school allows him to develop his talents and escape the grinding poverty of the orphanage but at a cost. He knows his sister thinks he has sold his humanity for the school.

Finally Werner is told he is eighteen, despite being sixteen, and sent to the front where he meets up with his protector, Volkheimer, from the school. Here they are in a unit of five men who track down partisan broadcasts and kill the men sending messages. This takes them over Europe including Austria where in Vienna a young girl is killed by mistake. Thus when they get to Saint-Malo Werner is vowed to protect the girl broadcasting science and reading a novel. Werner's experiences have altered him greatly. It is in Saint-Malo nearing the end of the war that the two meet, drawn together by radio waves and Marie-Laure is also changed: she has become the 'whelk'.

The war provides a broad setting for the novel which covers a lengthy period of time from 1934 to 2014. The war is a backdrop that allows the unconventional to happen and this is perfect for a novel that isn't a conventional war novel.

Questions on the setting

1. How Doerr portray Paris, both before and after the war? Explain your response with direct reference to *All the Light We Cannot See*.

2. Describe the *Museum National d'Histoire Naturelle*. For help the specific chapter starts on page 19

3. What qualities does Number 4 rue Vauborel have that make it interesting?

4. Discuss the impact of the war on Saint-Malo?

5. How does the environment seem to create an atmosphere of pessimism in Zollverein?

6. Comment on how Werner handles the *Jungmänner* (young men) he meets at school. How does he see most of them?

7. How does going from Zollverein to Berlin alter Jutta's life?

8. Do you think how Werner crosses Europe to get to Saint-Malo is realistic in the context of war?

CHARACTER ANALYSIS

Here we examine the major characters in the novel in terms of human experiences. The novel has many minor characters and if one specifically makes a point on human experiences that you wish to investigate please do so. Here I deal with the main participants in Doerr's novel.

Marie-Laure LeBlanc

Marie-Laure has some vision in her life before the cataracts take her sight away. She learns to adapt and the depth of her experiences are influenced by this disability. As we read and learn more about her character and inner strength she does become 'the whelk' with those appropriate characteristics. After initially struggling to adapt she manages to find her way about and gain more confidence. Doerr certainly creates a character that has much strength and the empathy with the reader is strong.

Marie-Laure is both limited and expanded by her disability. While she loses sight her other senses are expanded and she lives this way. She is able to exist quite comfortably in a small world like Saint-Malo and this allows her to engage with the world and have experiences as she does when she works with Madame Manec and the Resistance. This experience gives her confidence and she is able to manage sufficiently well to go to the grotto on her own.

This also exposes the narrowness of her ability as she has limited ability to deal with Von Rumpel who is hostile to her both at the grotto and when he is in her home at the end searching for the gem. These limitations don't make her any less competent just vulnerable and more engaging to the audience. She lives through her other senses and does well with them, especially after the war when she becomes more adept at going into the world. She travels with Etienne, forges a career in academia, has lovers and a child and is generally happy despite having some issues from the war;

> 'Marie-Laure still cannot wear shoes that are too large, or smell a boiled turnip, without experiencing revulsion. Neither can she listen to lists of names.' (p512)

The episodic way in which Marie-Laure is introduced to us is also interesting in that it builds a fragmented picture that Doerr can add to keep us interested as the narrative moves through different times and characters. Marie is 'a sightless sixteen year old' and then, 'a tall freckled six-year-old in Paris with rapidly deteriorating eyesight'. Doerr manages to add an element of mystery to keep us engaged with her character and follow her experiences throughout the course of the war.

Marie-Laure has some defining experiences that are extremely defining in situations that are extreme. She is taken from Paris, ends up in Saint-Malo, lives through the war, loses her father, works for the Resistance, is 'rescued' by Werner, deals with the gem, goes back to Paris and makes a new life, has a career, a child and a grandchild. It is by any definition a full life and a unique one. It certainly impacts on how she relates to the world and her attitudes towards life. She sacrifices the gem because of the way it brings (perhaps?) bad luck as told in the myth of the Sea of Flames.

Marie-Laure's life is interwoven in a complex manner with the world and some of the characters that Doerr creates. Her experiences cover a wide range of general human experiences but also some which are explicit to her. Her life is woven into a complex time in human history.

Werner Pfennig

Werner Pfennig is raised in 'a clinker-brick two-storey orphanage... whose rooms are populated with the coughs of sick children... (his) earliest years are the leanest.' He is;

> 'undersized and his ears stick out and he speaks with a high, sweet voice; the whiteness of his hair stops people in their tracks.' (p24)

Werner is brilliant at electronics and builds a radio which opens up a whole new world for him, 'the air streaming with possibility.' He uses this engineering and mathematical adeptness to make a different life for himself when his skill is recognised by Herr Seidler and he is sent to Schulpforta an elite school for the Reich. This is not what he expected and is a brutal introduction to the world of the Nazi Party. Here he learns of cruelty and they are forced to chant slogans. Here he learns about war and has to kill a prisoner.

Two positives emerge from this experience despite its bleakness of experience. For a while he has a friend in Frederick which allows him to see Berlin and experience a different aspect of life e.g. the restaurant and it also gives him the opportunity to meet Volkheimer through his work with Dr Hauptmann. Werner learns much here but also loses some of his humanity.

Later Werner, after surviving the war and his entombment in the cellar in Saint-Malo restores something in himself by aiding

Marie-Laure who he is connected to through the broadcasts he listened to as a child and her own readings and music. He hasn't reported her though he detected her signal and then kills Von Rumpel to save her. Werner's experiences are too much for him – he is a decent person and the war damages him. He dies by walking out into a minefield.

Werner too is evolved as a character by the war and his experiences in it are extreme. He is connected by the radio broadcasts initiated by Marie-Laure's grandfather and continued by Etienne and her. Werner sees and is accomplice to many bad things and these are things his sister warned him about. In the end his experiences destroy much of his humanity yet we do see glimpses of his decency such as the letter to the brain-damaged Frederick and his love for his sister.

Frank Volkheimer

Frank Volkheimer is a giant of a human;

> 'an upperclassman, seventeen years old, a colossal boy from some boreal village, a legend among the young cadets...There is a rumor that he crushed a communist's windpipe with his hands...They call him the Giant.' (p152)

Volkheimer is assigned to look out for Werner which gives him much kudos at school but this giant isn't all force, he has a love of music and is a more complex character. When the pair are reunited in the Ukraine Volkheimer again looks out for Werner and it is his resilience that gets them out of the cellar when all is seemingly lost.

After the war he lives in a 'third-floor walk-up in the suburb of Pforzheim, West Germany' and he is fifty-one years old in 1974. Volkheimer installs TV antennae so he isn't far away from his war time career. He does have an affection and remembrance for Werner as shown when he takes Werner's equipment to Jutta. Volkheimer is a complex character, not just a giant of a man. He is sensitive to classical music e.g. the way Marie-Laure's music stirs him to act when he is trapped in the cellar as it reminds him of 'the forest at dawn' when he was a child.

Daniel LeBlanc

Daniel is the locksmith at the Museum of Natural History and he is entrusted with the care of the jewel when they evacuate Paris. He manages to get to Saint-Malo with Marie-Laure and there he tries to build a new life. He is proud of his daughter and is caring and patient with her, 'He persists in asking Marie-Laure' to run her hands over the model and learn her way around.

When he is recalled to Paris he thinks of her and the future and rightly so because he is arrested by the Germans on the train, questioned and sent to a camp where he dies of pneumonia. He sends his daughter letters from the camp that are optimistic as not to worry her but they also contain the clue that leads her to the Sea of Flames hidden in the model house. Daniel is an excellent father and is a huge influence on Marie-Laure.

Etienne LeBlanc

Etienne is the link between Marie-Laure and Werner through the broadcasts of her grandfather, Henri, his brother. Etienne does not leave his house at Number 4 because of psychological issues from the First World War but is a kind loving man who takes Marie-Laure under his care, even more so after her father is taken by the Germans. He doesn't want to move out into the world but she eventually draws him out and in many ways saves him from the life he has created for himself.

The first step for Etienne is joining the Resistance and using his radio to broadcast messages before Marie-Laure goes missing and he ventures out;

> 'Now Etienne hyperventilates. At thirty-four minutes by his wristwatch, he puts on his shoes and a hat that belonged to his father. Stands in the foyer summoning all his resolve. When he last went out, almost twenty-four years ago, he tried to make eye contact, to present what might be considered a normal appearance. But the attacks were sly, unpredictable, devastating...He twists the latch, opens the gate. Steps outside.' (p417-8)

Later Etienne makes more of the world and adapts to life in Paris, selling the Saint-Malo house. He travels with Marie-Laure and dies 'gently in the bathtub at age eighty-two, and left her plenty of money.' Etienne changes and adapts to the experiences of his life and he is a good example of both experiences that have negative and positive impact.

Jutta Pfennig

Jutta is Werner's younger sister and she is sceptical of the Nazi regime as she listens to the radio for a range of information not just the Nazi propaganda. She doesn't want Werner to go to Schulpforta and is wary of his leaving. She later is forced to work for the German war effort and in Berlin is raped by three Russian soldiers with two other girls from the orphanage. Jutta writes Werner letters and he is often tardy in reply, not knowing what to tell her as he experiences things that she said would change him. In the end she learns of his death and tracks down Marie-Laure to return the model house. It has some kind of closure for her about a time she clearly wants to forget.

Madame Manec

Madame Manec is the housekeeper at Uncle Etienne's in Saint-Malo. She has been with him for years and when the LeBlanc's arrive;

> 'she seems short; she wears blocky, heavy shoes. Hers is a low voice, full of pebbles – a sailor's voice or a smoker's.'
> (p120)

She is a feisty old lady and actively works for the Resistance against the 'Boche'. She is later to die of pneumonia after seeming to recover and Etienne is devastated but it does motivate him to re-engage with the world.

Frederick

Frederick is Werner's only true friend and he is from a wealthy Berlin family. He and Werner share a holiday together in Frederick's Berlin apartment and this gives Werner a taste of a different life, even the elevator being a new experience. Frederick is a boy of intriguing character who is focused on birds. He sees the world as it is and his refusal to participate in the torture of a prisoner makes him a bullying victim. Already small and physically weak he is eventually beaten so badly he has brain damage. He lives out the rest of his life disabled with his mother drawing spirals and not recognising much of the world around him.

Reinhold von Rumpel

Von Rumpel is a sergeant major in the Wehrmacht and his job is to value and send back to Germany confiscated valuables. He is extremely ill with tumours that will eventually kill him and has a limp by which Marie-Laure recognises him. His aim is to find the Sea of Flames because it is part of the myth that the stone makes the owner immortal. He is a figure who uses and abuses his power and has no sentiment at all except for the small episode where he thinks of his family. He is eventually killed by Werner before he can find Marie-Laure in the house.

Dr Hauptmann

The doctor is the man who takes Werner under his wing at Schulpforta and teaches him deep skills in mechanics and trigonometry. They work together at the school successfully until Hauptmann is transferred to Berlin where he is to continue his studies. He tells Werner;

> 'We live in exceptional times, cadet.' (p154)

and tells Werner that he will work in the laboratory every night after dinner. Eventually he lies to the staff about Werner's age so he is drafted into the Wehrmacht.

Frau Elena

She is the Protestant nun who runs the orphanage that Werner and Jutta grow up in. she is a good woman who does her best for the children and encourages, within her means, the children to succeed. Her life is difficult and tedious and she has little means but manages to keep the children alive. Importantly her wider experience gives the children both German and French which helps Werner when he communicates with Marie-Laure.

Questions on Character

1. Why does Daniel LeBlanc have to leave Paris and generate some new experiences? Is he thinking of himself or does he also have Marie-Laure in mind? How does he plan for the future? What impression do you have of him from here until we find out about his death?

2. Discuss the effect of Marie-Laure losing her sight as a child on the narrative.

3. How do you see Uncle Etienne? Discuss how he changes through the course of the narrative and how THREE specific experiences change how he sees the world and/or his attitude to it.

4. Analyse the role of Werner in *All the Light We Cannot See* in terms of the human experience. Think about the way in which he contributes to the emotions, ideas and assumptions different characters make.

5. Explain the role of the Madame Manec in the narrative. How does she enhance change? What types of conflict does she add to the narrative?

6. While we are focused on human experiences as our main idea we also need to think about other concepts that integrate into this idea. I think the novel is also about relationships in their various forms. Do you agree with this thought? Explain your ideas with specific reference *All the Light We Cannot See*. Specifically comment on how the characters become interwoven.

7. Describe how Von Rumpel comes to focus on the Sea of Flames. Why are his experiences that impel him to find the gem? What do you think about his character?

8. What role does Volkheimer play in the narrative? Why do you think Doerr brings him back in 1974 and tells us about his life and includes him in the resolution?

9. Who would you say is the antagonist of *All the Light We Cannot See*? Perhaps there are multiple ones at different stages?

10. Discuss ONE minor character. Analyse the reasons for your decisions about including that character and discuss what role you think they play in *All the Light We Cannot See*.

11. Discuss ONE other character not mentioned in this analysis and state what contribution they make to our understanding and appreciation of *All the Light We Cannot See*.

THEMATIC CONCERNS

Human Experiences in *All the Light We Cannot See*

It is always important to go back to the rubric before setting off in an examination of *All the Light We Cannot See*. Think specifically what you are looking for and how the novel conveys the human experience. I have commented on explicit human experiences in the summary of the narrative but here I will explore some of the broader sweeps that Doerr creates in an examination of human experiences in the text.

The war is a huge landscape for the narrative to unfold as we move across Europe. For Marie-Laure the move from Paris to Saint-Malo is long and traumatic as she is experiencing new things at a dramatic rate as the world changes around her. For Werner too, we see great change from the orphanage to his selective school environment. Doer manages to weave these experiences into a tapestry that links characters across time and geography. It is not only these individual experiences that are undertaken. Think of the collective experiences of the peoples involved in the war and even at the town or village level. The war affects whole groups and many of these experiences are negative – think of the deaths, the camps, the shortages and the rapes as examples.

We see the full gamut of human emotions as well due to the stresses and excesses of war. We see people – who might otherwise be 'good' people – do horrible things, we see inconsistencies in behaviour and we see people continue to be the person they are. One example of this is 'Big Claude' who is always rather cunning and he is an individual who thrives off the war. Frederick is the opposite of this with his ethical basis for living and appreciation of beauty. His consistency leaves him alienated in a world of paradoxes and he is a loner, beaten and damaged by the war. Jutta, too, sees the inconsistencies in the German propaganda because she is aware, through the overseas broadcasts, of the atrocities committed by the Nazis. Each of the characters has different motivations and takes a different view of the world because of the war.

If we examine a character who the war benefits because of his changing place in the world Von Rumpel is a good example. Before the Nazis he was a gemmologist of low ethical standards, the perfect person for a place in the Nazi regime. He is able to not even consider the morality of the Nazi theft and indeed is motivated to do anything to find the Sea of Flames. His lack of moral fibre is perfect for his character but we also see the contrast when he thinks of his family – one act that makes him human.

Other characters that do have a defined vision of themselves in the world move through the war solidified by these assumptions. Daniel LeBlanc is all about his work and his daughter. He doesn't allow the war and his own personal circumstance to deflect him from these things – despite it costing him his life in a camp. Madame Manec uses her experiences to solidify her contempt for the Germans and work for the resistance despite her age.

Marie-Laure and Werner also develop and change their ideas about life through their experiences during the war. We see Werner, who dreams of a life away from his home town and orphanage not get what he expects despite him sacrificing his own standards as his sister expected him to do because of the circumstances at Schulpforta. Werner's experiences lead directly to his demise and the wide-eyed innocent, intelligent boy has gone. He manages to redeem his moral basis at the end by 'saving' Marie-Laure and killing von Rumpel but even this doesn't manage to help his psyche. The stories and lectures that he hears on the radio aren't enough to sustain him but they do save Marie-Laure.

Marie-Laure uses the broadcasts to sustain herself through the bombing and the intrusion of von Rumpel into her house. They are also used to assist the French Resistance in the underground war against the 'Boche'. Marie-Laure becomes very adept at surviving. She takes on the persona of the 'whelk';

> '"How about the Whelk?' I think I would like to be the Whelk."' (p266)

This idea allows her to endure as we see near the conclusion of the novel when she is alone and vulnerable,

> 'She thinks of the whelks in Hubert Bazin's kennel, ten thousand of them; how they cling; how they draw themselves up into the spirals of their shells; how, when they're tucked into that grotto, the gulls cannot come in to carry them up into the sky and drop them on the rocks to break them.' (p446)

The music and the stories that Marie-Laure plays and her grandfather before her are experiences that cross all cultural boundaries and bind people across experiences. The music saves Volkheimer, the science recordings give Werner hope as a child and the story brings them together. This goes to show us that the concept of stories is integrated into all cultures and can reach across differences – especially political ones. These stories affect people individually and emotionally as well as intellectually yet they are also able to have an effect collectively on the human consciousness.

For Werner to be with Marie-Laure in the room where the broadcasts were made was 'like medicine' and he thinks 'I only want to sit here with her for a thousand hours.' He thinks there are 'wonders' in the house and gently keeps a page from *Birds of America* for Frederick. Werner never makes it back to what Volkheimer said, *'What you could be'* but he does have a range of experiences before he dies that lead to the moment he steps on the mine. Before he dies Werner thinks of the simpler, innocent moments of his life with Jutta, experiences that mean something to him. He doesn't have new ideas now; he clings to the past as a reassuring image.

The human experiences in *All the Light We Cannot See* don't always end positively but this is the reality of the human experience. Marie-Laure manages to forge a life after the war but she has the scars of her experiences and isn't always happy. Etienne seems to have three distinct lives based around the two wars and is able to change his behaviour and motivations to reflect a changing world and his own personal needs.

Certainly the human experiences in *All the Light We Cannot See* are defined by the experiences of the war. It allows some people to change, in others it reinforces characteristics while others are unable to survive. It is interesting to think that the two individuals most disabled i.e. Marie-Laure and Etienne seem to be the ones that adapt best and change to the circumstances thrust upon them. Whether this intentional on Doerr's part is debatable but it is an interesting aspect of his understanding of human experiences.

Now we will have a look at some questions to define these idea and develop specific examples.

Questions on Human Experiences

1. Define the term human experiences in your own words and apply this definition to *All the Light We Cannot See*.

2. Name TWO images that contribute to the audiences understanding and enjoyment of the text and state what they contribute to the experience of one or more characters.

3. Discuss the effect of wartime experiences that impact on THREE characters and how it changed an attitude or way in which they interact with the world.

4. How do experiences prior to the war affect how TWO characters navigate the complex experiences of the war? Discuss how these experiences change how the character sees the world during wartime and/or his attitude to it.

5. Analyse the role of disability in *All the Light We Cannot See* in terms of the human experience. Think about the way in which he contributes to the emotions, ideas and assumptions different characters make. For example Frederick's eyesight, Etienne's post-traumatic stress or Von Rumpel's cancer.

6. Explain the role of the radio broadcasting in the narrative. How does it enhance change? What types of conflict does it add to the narrative?

7. Human experiences in the text show us the extremes of human nature. Do you agree with this statement? Explain your ideas with specific reference *All the Light We Cannot See*.

8. Another thought that critics suggest Doerr alludes to is that of the 'moral obligation'. Do you agree with this idea? Explain your response fully and then analyse what Doerr is saying about these obligations.

9. In a book that focuses on the war as its setting how does Doerr convey emotions and attitudes in a convincing manner?

10. Discuss ONE idea in *All the Light We Cannot See* that hasn't been discussed here that YOU think is relevant to our understanding of the text in terms of understanding the human experience.

11. Do you consider *All the Light We Cannot See* to be a good example of the representation of the human experience? Does it also offer something wider than this narrow view?

LANGUAGE TECHNIQUES IN *ALL THE LIGHT WE CANNOT SEE*

Doerr's episodic narrative takes us across time and a continent. The narrative isn't chronological but bounces back and forward until the characters and ideas unite at the time the Americans free Saint-Malo with some after thoughts until the present. The third-person omniscient narration follows different threads of the narrative and covers a vast amount of time and experiences for each of the characters.

The idea of light in the novel draws upon aspects of the different characters and the blindness of Marie-Laure. The references to light are frequent and often defining. For Marie-Laure her 'Congenital cataracts' won't allow her to 'see anything for the rest of her life. Werner's last thought for example is 'Why doesn't the wind move the light' and the light we cannot see can be defined as the legacy of people and the good that they do. There are other interpretations that have been offered as we shall see later but this is simple and easily supported.

I have already discussed the idea of Marie-Laure taking on the characteristics of the 'Whelk' but the symbolism of her struggle against darkness and the odds is critical to the success of the novel. Another success for Doerr's style is just inherent in the idea of writing something new about such a well-worn topic as World War Two but he does draw new ideas and offers individual experiences as a story about the common humanity in us and how it can be lost and/ or gained in moments of great change and significance.

Another concept you might like to think about is the idea of the radio waves and how they link people. Doerr makes this quite explicit in the final section 2014 when Marie-Laure is in the park with her grandson, Max,

'Marie-Laure imagines the electromagnetic waves travelling... just as Etienne used to describe, except now a thousand times more crisscross the air than when he lived – maybe a million times more...And is it so hard to believe that souls might also travel those paths? That her father and Etienne and Madame Manec and the German boy named Werner Pfennig might harry the skies in flocks...and the record of every life lived, every sentence spoken, every words transmitted still reverberating within it.' (p529)

Doerr's style is certainly full of imagery and long descriptive passages that are complex but he balances this with short episodes to give the reader some time to think and appreciate what is happening. This also applies to the narrative which does switch about. His style has both critics and advocates so let's have a deeper look at this aspect.

The novel has mixed critical reception and we will examine some of the analyses over the next few pages. Let's begin positively and remember that you don't have to agree or disagree with what critics think but have arguments to support or refute ideas. Now let's see what others think of Doerr's style and language,

Amanda Veill says in *The Washington Post*,

'I'm not sure I will read a better novel this year than Anthony Doerr's "All the Light We Cannot See." Enthrallingly told, beautifully written and so emotionally plangent that some passages bring tears, it is completely unsentimental

— no mean trick when you consider that Doerr's two protagonists are children who have been engulfed in the horror of World War II. Not martyred emblems, like Anne Frank or the British evacuees on the torpedoed City of Benares, just ordinary children, two of thousands swallowed up in a conflict they had nothing to do with.'

www.washingtonpost.com/entertainment/books/all-the-light-we-cannot-see-by-anthony-doerr/2014/05/05/c2deec58-cf14-11e3-a6b1-45c4dffb85a6_story.html

Another positive analysis of the novel can be found in the *New Yorker,*

'The dual protagonists of this gripping novel, set during the Second World War, are the blind daughter of a Parisian locksmith who builds an intricate model of the streets to help her navigate her world and a German orphan whose uncanny aptitude for mechanics makes him valuable to the Nazi war effort. Doerr's plotting is intricate, and he shifts effectively between the two stories. There are also chapters from the point of view of a Nazi gemmologist who is scouring Europe for an invaluable diamond. As the strands of the plot converge, the book becomes a meditation on fate, free will, and the way that, in wartime, small choices can have vast consequences.'

http://www.newyorker.com/magazine/2014/06/23/briefly-noted-758

In a more critical analysis of Doerr's work Dominic Green in the *New Republic* says,

'Moreover, Doerr's writing is pompous, pretentious, and imprecise. Every noun is escorted by an adjective of reliable but uninspiring quality. Eyes are "wounded." Brown hair is "mousy." Absurdly, Wehrmacht recruits are "greyhounds, harvested from all over the nation for their speed and eagerness to obey." I always thought greyhounds were bred, not picked like fruit. But then, I'm not a scientist. And neither is Doerr. He clutters his novel with technological whimsy about time, speed, and connectedness. Every event, especially a fatal one, is "destined" for reasons too mysterious and complex to explain. Science is an object of gawping wonder, but its merits remain beyond description, venerated but incommunicable.'

https://newrepublic.com/article/120769/problem-anthony-doerrs-all-light-we-cannot-see

Again we can make these criticisms of the style of the novel as Justin Cartwright does in *The Guardian*,

'Of course as you read the dual story, you wonder how soon it is before Marie-Laure and Werner are going to meet. And it is a weakness of this book that it has many aspects of genre fiction, despite the huge amount of research that has gone into it. There is a worrying even-handedness in Doerr's treatment of the Germans and the French. There are also some strange mistakes: for instance, Niels Bohr was not a German. However, the story itself is gripping and it is easy to understand why Doerr's book is regarded by many as an epic and a masterpiece.'

https://www.theguardian.com/books/2015/may/17/all-light-we-cannot-see-review-anthony-doerr-pulitzer-prize

Now we have read what impressions there are of the novel we can do some questions to refine these ideas and develop our own understanding.

Questions on Techniques

1. Give TWO specific examples of human experiences and the techniques Doerr uses to convey that image.

2. Why is important to create picture images in the readers mind in a novel such as *All the Light We Cannot See*. Think about the character of Marie-Laure and the context of the novel for modern audiences.

3. Find THREE descriptions that use at least four of the five senses. Why might an author such as Doerr focus on using the senses to engage readers?

4. Comment on the use of one specific language technique used in *All the Light We Cannot See* and analyse its effect in the novel.

5. Do you think the 'Whelk' is an apt description of Marie-Laure? Explain your response with direct reference to *All the Light You Cannot See*.

6. How does the light feature as a motif in Doerr's work? Explain your response with the inclusion of direct quotes.

7. What particular importance do the radio waves have in the narrative? Think not just about the specific waves but what they imply and how they draw the narrative together.

8. Select ONE description in *All the Light You Cannot See* and show, by annotation, how Doerr creates a picture in the reader's mind.

9. Describe one image in the narrative that particularly struck you and why how it influenced you.

10. Discuss ONE of the critical analyses that you have read here. What does it add to your understanding of *All the Light You Cannot See*?

11. If you had the opportunity to add a new episode to *All the Light You Cannot See* what would it be and where in the novel would you place it. Try and write the outline and discuss why it is relevant to the human experience(s) in the novel.

THE ESSAY

The essay consists of the basic form of an introduction, body paragraphs and conclusion. The esssay has been the subject of numerous texts and you should have the basic form well in hand. As teachers, the point we would emphasise would be to link the paragraphs both to each other and back to your argument (which should directly respond to the question). Of course, ensure your argument is logical and sustained.

Make sure you use specific examples and that your quotes are accurate. To ensure that you respond to the question, make sure you plan carefully and are sure what relevant point each paragraph is making. It is solid technique to actually 'tie up' each point by explicitly coming back to the question.

When composing an essay the basic conventions of the form are:

> - State your argument, outline the points to be addressed and perhaps have a brief definition.

↓

> **A solid structure for each paragraph is:**
> - Topic sentence (*the main idea and its link to the previous paragraph/ argument*)
> - Explanation/ discussion of the point including links between texts if applicable.
> - Detailed evidence (*Close textual reference – quotes, incidents and technique discussion.*)
> - Tie up by restating the point's relevance to argument/ question

↓

> - Summary of points
> - Final sentence that restates your argument

As well as this basic structure, you will need to focus on:

Audience – for the essay the audience must be considered formal unless specifically stated otherwise. Therefore, your language must reflect the audience. This gives you the opportunity to use the jargon and vocabulary that you have learnt in English. For the audience ensure your introduction is clear and has impact. Avoid slang or colloquial language including contractions (like doesn't', 'e.g.', 'etc.').

Purpose – the purpose of the essay is to answer the question given. The examiner evaluates how well you can make an argument and understand the module's issues and its text(s). An essay is solidly structured so its composer can analyse ideas. This is where you earn marks. It does not retell the story or state the obvious.

Communication – Take a few minutes to plan the essay. If you rush into your answer it is almost certain you will not make the most of the brief 40 minutes to show all you know about the question. More likely you will include irrelevant details that do not gain you marks but waste your precious time. Remember an essay is formal so **do not** do the following: story-tell, list and number points, misquote, use slang or colloquial language, be vague, use non-sentences or fail to address the question.

PLAN:

Don't even think about starting without one!

> *Introduce...*
> the texts you are using in the response
> *Argument*: The human experience is affected by:
> - Idea One
> - Idea Two
> - Idea Three

You need to let the marker know what texts you are discussing. You can start with a definition but it can come in the first paragraph of the body. You MUST state your argument in response to the question and the points you will cover as part of it. Wait until the end of the response to give it!

> **Idea One** – Aspect of human experience as outlined in the textual material, e.g. physical impact.
>
> **Idea Two** – Another aspect of human experience as outlined in the textual material, e.g. psychological impact.
> - explain the idea
> - where and how is it shown in the prescribed text?
> - where and how is it shown in related text 1?
>
> **Idea Three** – People's sense of experience is affected by context and environment
> - explain the idea
> - where and how shown in the prescribed text?
> - where and how shown in related text 1?

You can use the things you have learned to organise the essay. For each one, you say where you saw this in your prescribed text and where in related text(s).

Two or three ideas are usually enough as you can explore them in detail.

> - Summary of two key ideas
> - Final sentence that restates your argument

Make sure your conclusion restates your argument. It does not have to be too long.

© Five Senses Education Pty Ltd

MODEL ESSAY OUTLINE

> **To what extent are human experiences significant in the set text?**
>
> **From your studies respond to this question using your set text and at ONE piece of other textual material**

This essay needs to be attacked in a manner that responds to the question and shows ALL your knowledge about the text. The question lends itself to a close study of Anthony Doerr's *All the Light We Cannot See* as the text does show how the human experience is integral to life and how it shapes our other experiences and interaction with the world.

An introduction might be written:

> Human experiences are important in Doerr's novel *All the Light We Cannot See* and the two related texts Lawrence's film *Jindabyne* and Ed Sheeran's song *Castle on the Hill*. These texts show how human experiences are integral to human existence and bring more meaning to one's life. Life is about experiences that challenge us and define how we see the world. They shape our beliefs and attitudes and can be confronting at the same time. Without experiences our lives would be empty and meaningless.

Your essay should then follow the outlined plan and develop these ideas. This gives you the opportunity to link the texts and fully develop each of the ideas.

ANNOTATED RELATED MATERIAL: DIFFERENT STUDIES OF HUMAN EXPERIENCES

Jindabyne – Ray Lawrence

Jindabyne is an Australian film that captures a wide array of human experiences. It touches on the ideas mentioned in the introduction to this text in a number of detailed instances. We can begin by considering the following before beginning a detailed examination of the narrative.

The collective human experience:

- Aboriginality and the spiritual;
- The Fishermen and their code;
- The reaction of the townsfolk;
- Media response;
- Interaction with the natural world.

Individual Experience:

- An individual character's response to the body – choose one;
- The killer;
- Response to the revelations;
- Past experiences and how they impact on current experiences;
- Reaction to loss – emotional;
- Assumptions about life.

We can now look at the plot to help us understand each of these issues. *Jindabyne* begins with the sound of a radio being tuned and the Australian feel of the movie is immediate with the theme music for the ABC news. Lawrence emphasises the isolation by having the radio not tune in correctly for an unknown female character, forcing her to use the cassette player. With this unusual beginning we know that her experience is not going to be positive.

We then pan to the rocks slowly where Gregory, our killer, sits patiently in a truck with the engine running watching the road. We know he is prepared for this as he has binoculars. He sees an Aboriginal girl, Susan O'Connor, driving and she is the one fiddling with the radio. He chases her down and forces her to stop. He moves toward her as we see a long shot of how isolated they are. We see his face in her window looming above her and screaming about the electricity coming down from the mountains. This film is no murder mystery, as we know from the beginning that the murderer is Gregory the electrician. This is about the experiences of the other characters in the film and how they respond to current experiences.

The Kane family, Stewart, Claire and son Tom, is waking. Claire pretends to sleep, before waking suddenly and being affectionate with Tom. Stewart and Tom head out fishing. The scene doesn't feel quite right and there is some emotional tension between Stewart and Claire that is unspoken due to what they have experienced in the past. Claire had a complicated past when she was pregnant with Tom. When she finds she is pregnant again, she becomes emotional and slightly unstable.

As the film builds we see the complex pasts of the characters and their interactions in the confinement of the small town. The fishing trip is a break from this and extremely important in their lives.

We see some of the emotional instability in characters such as Caylin-Calandria, who with Tom, has some issues at school Along with Caylin-Calandria, Claire and Jude also have issues but in a nicely framed shot of the three female characters, we see them conform as members of a close knit group. The sacrifice they make is similar to Gregory's but on a different scale. Note the connection here and how each one is to get back to order and societal norms. This is the collective experience for all the characters.

At the Kanes' home the tensions are obvious from their past experiences but they contain it for appearances' sake. Occasionally, the tension reaches breaking point and the experience strains the superficial approach. The tension builds at home and the fishing trip seems like a good opportunity to break the cycle.

When we see Gregory dump Susan O'Connor's body in the river, we know that the fishing and her death will interact.

The next morning, the fishermen head off for their one big trip of the year and the sign 'Gone fishing' is put in the garage window. We see Billy on the phone to Elissa and putting the sign the wrong way round in the window shows his immaturity. They have already said they are taking him away to make a man of him. The four men have a few beers on the way and talk as they travel through the landscape. They intend to give Billy the experience they think he needs as a 'man' — a cultural rite of passage.

The men arrive and the high-tension electricity wires punctuate the wilderness. They begin to hike toward the valley. It's a long walk in and the terrain is hilly and difficult. They stop on the way and again we see Billy's naivety when Stewart says 'Listen to that' meaning the silence but he can't, as he has his earphones in. It is part of the break in tension of the film that they commune with nature. This experiential break affects all the men. The episode represents a distinct human experience.

Stewart wanders down the river fishing and sees Susan's body caught in the rocks. Hesitantly, he wades out to it and turns it over saying 'Oh Jesus' repeatedly. He screams for the others to come as he drags the body to the bank. He is obviously upset, making the sign of the cross. Stewart tells Rocco to 'take her, for fuck's sake, take her' and their shock is obvious. They all stare at the body and Billy goes to run off but they stop him. The four men meet and decide to leave her in the water and tie her so she doesn't float away.

The presence of the body threatens to detract from the enjoyment of the fishing experience. The act of attempted isolation of the bad experience is expected to evoke only a mild response. They do not anticipate the stormy reaction it receives when they return to the community.

The men go on fishing, with Stewart getting the first big fish on an absolutely perfect day. The lure of the fish is strong, especially when they see the big one he has caught. They have a successful and enjoyable time, a positive experience. They get a photo of the catch and Billy holds up his fish in a typical hunter/gatherer pose. Capturing an experience this way is most enjoyable.

It is a photo that will come back to haunt them as things change back in the world. An unanticipated adverse reaction can be a horrific experience.

Stewart goes to check on the dead girl, rolling her over and getting debris off her face in a quite tender gesture. The next day they head back and report it. At the car Billy rings Elissa and says they found a body but 'caught the most amazing fish'. They are told by the police to wait and seem despondent their trip has been ruined. They organise their story as Stewart says they have 'to get their story straight'.

We cut to Gregory eating breakfast and he appears to be a normal lonely man until he goes out to his shed where he has hidden Susan's car and this reminds us of the evil in him. Consider his experience and his motivations. How does he see his actions and the world?

The next day at the station the policeman tells the fishermen 'we don't step over bodies for our recreational pursuits' and 'the whole town's ashamed of you'. When they are told to 'piss off' from the station the press are waiting for them and Billy makes a comment. Carl is angry with the press but we can begin to see signs of distress within the whole group.

The experience they had so looked forward to has become a negative one and the tensions we saw before are exacerbated by the emotional and collective response to the murder. Claire soon becomes obsessed with the whole affair because of her own state. The newspaper the next day has the headline, 'Men fish over dead body' because Billy has talked. Billy is late to work and Stewart tells him they have to 'stick together on this'.

Susan's sister calls them 'animals' and raises the race question by asking if they would have left a white girl. The Aboriginal youths begin to attack and vandalise the property of the men in violent outbursts, including throwing a rock through Billy's van window and thus endangering his baby. They insult Carl at the caravan park and vandalise the garage.

The police aren't any help and the situation deteriorates. Jude tells the police they shouldn't be enforcing the 'political correctness' laws. The intervention of the sense of Aboriginality and race challenges the assumptions people have and how we see the world. The contrasting views are ingrained in the social structures and part of different collective experiences.

The Aboriginal people see the white people as 'interfering' and the group of fishermen begin to fight amongst themselves. Elissa says they shouldn't go to the bush at all as it's sacred. The group talk about the bush and Rocco punches Stewart for saying the Aborigines are superstitious. The experience of racial tension becomes ever-present and adds to the emotional responses to the experience.

We now head slowly to a resolution of the conflict brought about by the various experiences. Each is handled in a different manner by characters and you can explore one or two of the responses. To cycle back to the original murder, Claire is stalked by Gregory in his truck. He stops her but drives off after staring weirdly, an odd experience in itself.

Terry and Stewart talk and Stewart meets Rocco and Carl. He tells them Claire's left him 'again'. Rocco can't believe it and we cross cut to her looking out into the wilderness after he looks thoughtfully out the window. These different reactions to experiences mirror attitudes in life and reactions to emotional and intellectual conflict.

In conclusion, Lawrence takes us back to the healing power of nature in our human experiences when the Aboriginal people are having a ceremony. Gregory watches while Claire walks in. Again we see his truck as an omnipresent force in the film, almost an extension of him. An Aboriginal man tells Claire to 'piss off' from the ceremony after she says she has come to pay her 'respects' but he is told to leave her alone by an Auntie.

The smoke and tribal music symbolise the ceremonial nature of the setting and the camera pans around the scene and the bush. We see parts of the ceremony with chanting and clapping sticks. The camera moves in and out while other shots pan around the bush, giving us the full experience and Lawrence portrays this as a positive, healing experience.

Eventually Stewart, Tom, Carl, Jude and Rocco arrive to pay respects. Tom runs to his mother and Stewart goes over and says 'Sorry' but is rebuffed by the father who throws dirt on him and spits, refusing his apology. Then an Aboriginal girl tells a little about Susan's story and sings the last love song Susan wrote.

The camera pans around all the faces as they listen to the song and the ceremonial smoke wafts around. It seems to have some healing effect on everyone, as it is a meaningful experience which raises the idea of the spiritual experience in the text. The girl stops singing through emotion. 'Be gone' seems to symbolise in language the whole scenario for each character.

We see a long wide shot of the bush before fading back to Gregory waiting again in his car behind the rocks for another victim. It is quite a circular conclusion and it is an odd end when he crushes the fly. We don't quite know what to make of the whole experience and he seems to be the only character unchanged by the experiences in the film.

Poem: 'Inland' by John Kinsella

The poem captures the mood and ethos of the outback farming communities and deals with the human aspect more than some of the other poems in Kinsella's collection: *Peripheral Light*. This poem is one long restless thought that mimics memories and recollection while raising the current, topical issues that concern the poet. As usual with his poems Kinsella orientates the audience early with the word 'Inland' and then continues the poem without a full stop. The poem flows with the use of commas but Kinsella allows us to stop and think with the use of the colon, brackets and the hyphen. Look for these punctuation stops as you read as they emphasise a specific point or idea that resonates with the audience.

The first stanza gives us a foreshadowing of the events to follow with the warnings in the words 'storm', 'alert' and 'uncertain'. This ominous tone is reinforced by the word 'ghosts' and the implication of death which is constant in much of Kinsella's poetry. The next stanza deals with a more human element and we get the country feel with the bracketed gossip about McHenry's accident which shows the close knit community. Habits here are formed as part of survival and known to all as we see 'the old man plying the same track' and the families possibly heading to church on the Sunday morning.

The third stanza returns to the vagaries of nature. Kinsella repeats 'uncertain' with regard to the weather. Weather and the environment play a large role in farming communities and it is especially so at sowing and harvest. Despite the uncertainty and 'ashen' days which alter 'moods', the community returns to their habits and routines which shape their lives. The next stage returns to the road and the implication of a journey but a journey that is straight and in conflict with the cycles of the natural world The path seems already marked and measured. It is 'straight and narrow', marked by a theodolite.

The final four lines of the poem are pure Kinsella, marking the transience of humanity on the landscape. We read

> 'it's a place of borrowed dreams
> where the marks of the spirit
> have been erased by dust –
> the restless topsoil'

The European farmers had 'borrowed dreams' for their own relationship with the land but this line also harks back to the indigenous Dreamtime when the land was created. The indigenous view that the land owns the people is also true for Kinsella. This sense of nobody owning the land is strong in his poetry. European impact on the land can be seen in the spirituality being removed by the dust—dust created by the poor farming techniques transferred from a different land. He finishes with the 'restless topsoil' as if the whole earth is moving in its own discontented journey, just as the people move.

The influence here of genuinely lost spirituality and connection with the land as we move directly on the 'high road' contrasts with the more flowing, 'restless' side of the natural world. This visual contrast is obvious but we can also discuss the contrast between habit and spirit. 'Inland' is a poem that uses the landscape to show the contrast between two views of the countryside.

DRAMA: Eugene O'Neil's *Desire Under the Elms*

O'Neill sets out to instruct how the house and elms should appear and the year is 1850. Note how he describes the 'enormous' elms as,

> 'exhausted women resting their sagging breasts and
> hands and hair on its roof, and when it rains their tears
> trickle down monotonously and rot on the shingles'

and how they dominate and 'rot'. It is important to read this both in terms of the play and in the context of American theatre. The description here shows O'Neill's genius at new design and original theatricality.

Part One: Scene One

The whole first page and a third are nearly all playwright notes that describe the farm, the house and the characters of Eben, Simeon and Peter. The first words of the play, 'God! Purty!' reflect the beauty of the land and how Eben perceives it. Eben is 'resentful and defensive' and feels 'trapped' on the farm.

His older half-brothers Simeon and Peter are 'more bounce and homelier in face, shrewder and more practical.' They all have worked hard on their father's farm over the years and have little feeling for their absent father. We learn that Simeon had a 'woman' who died and that Peter is excited by the prospect of 'gold in the West'. They all talk about how hard they've worked and hope that the father might 'die soon'. What we get from all this is that they are earthy and this is reflected in their bodies and clothes which are all dirt stained.

We also see here the difference between them as Eben sees gold in the pasture, not California, as they head in for a dinner of bacon in what seems a ritual they have performed many times before. Note that O'Neill calls for the use of the curtain at the end of the scene.

Scene Two

It is twilight and again we get detailed notes on the interior scene. Simeon tells Eben he should not wish their father dead and Eben replies he's not his son but, 'I'm Maw – every drop of blood!' He then blames the father, Ephraim Cabot, for killing his mother by working her to death but the others just say there was work to be done. O'Neill gets them to list the jobs and Eben comes back with 'vengeful passion' that, while they did nothing, he will see his mother gets 'rest and sleep in her grave!'

They then discuss Cabot's absence and how he just drove off in a buggy one day in a rush. Simeon says that when he went,

> 'He druv off in the buggy, all spick an' span, with the mare all breshed an' shiny, druv off clackin' his tongue an' wavin' his whip. I remember it quite well'

Eben mocks Simeon for not stopping him and the scene concludes with Eben leaving to see Minnie the town whore. We learn all the Cabot men have slept with her. Simeon and Peter say that Eben is just like 'Paw' and thinks of California. The final image is of Eben with his arms stretched to the sky talking about starts and sin, 'my sin's as purty as any one on 'em!', until he 'strides' to the village for Min.

Scene Three

It is 'pitch darkness' and Eben comes home with the news that Cabot has married a 'purty' thirty-five year old. He has heard this in the village and this effectively disinherits the boys. Simeon and Peter see California as their only option now. Eben tells the boys that they can have three hundred dollars each if they sign their share of the farm over to him. He can get the money as his mother told him,

> 'I know whar it's hid. I been waitin' – Maw told me. She knew whar it lay fur years, but she was waitin'....It's her'n – the money he hoarded from her farm an' hid from Maw. It's my money by rights now.'

They think about it and Eben tells them about his night with Min. He tells how he hates the new wife after the boys suggest he might sleep with her, just like Min, to get the old man back. Peter and Simeon say they'll do the deal and leave the farm. Both are bitter and vindictive about Cabot.

Scene Four

The setting is the same as Scene Two and the boys are discussing how they don't have to work now – it is all down to Eben who is jubilant as he thinks it will all be his. Peter and Simeon again reflect on how like his father he is, 'Like his Paw'. They also tell he isn't much of a milker but they soon talk about their leaving and how they'll miss some aspects of the farm.

Eben comes back in and says that the 'old mule an the bride' are coming. The two older boys begin to pack and sign Eben's papers as he gives them the money Cabot had hidden. They tell him they'll send him 'a lump o' gold for Christmas' and head into the yard feeling 'light' because of their newfound freedom.

Ephraim Cabot and Abbie Putnam then come in and O'Neill describes them in detail. Cabot is

> 'seventy-five, tall and gaunt, with great, wiry, concentrated power, but stoop shouldered by toil. His face is hard as if it were hewn from a boulder, yet there is a weakness in it'

but his face is weakened with petty pride. Abbie is

> 'thirty-five, buxom, full of vitality. Her round face is pretty but marred by its rather gross sensuality. There is strength and obstinacy in her jaw, a hard determination in her eyes, and about her whole personality.'

She also has a 'desperate quality'. Cabot shows Abbie the place and she says to him it's 'mine'. Then he sees the two boys not working. He introduces Abbie and she goes to look at 'her' house and they warn her Eben's inside.

Cabot tells them to get to work and they give him cheek, saying they are 'free' and heading to California. They 'whoop' it up and he says he'll have them chained up. They throw rocks at the house, smashing the window and head off singing. Abbie sticks her head out the window and says she likes the room but he is thinking of the stock and 'almost runs' to the barn.

Abbie then meets Eben in the kitchen and talks to him in 'seductive tones'. She says she doesn't want to be his 'Maw' but friends and he cusses her. She tells him of her troubled life and how Cabot gave her a chance to escape it. He calls her a 'harlot' and they argue over ownership of the farm. She has the upper hand in law and he leaves but the seeds of their growing attraction have been set.

Outside he and his father argue about life and work and he tells Eben 'Ye'll never be more'n half a man!' The scene ends with Abbie washing up and the faint notes of the song the boys were singing as they left.

Part Two: Scene One

Again O'Neill describes in detail the farmhouse setting. Two months have passed and it is a hot Sunday afternoon. Abbie in her best outfit is sitting on the porch and Eben comes out of the house also dressed in his best. They stalk each other, both attracted and repelled. As he walks away she 'gives a sneering, taunting chuckle' at him and they argue but the attraction is obvious. She says that nature will pull him to her but he says that she is married and he goes to leave her.

She accuses him of going to Min and she gets angry stating he'll never get the farm,

> 'Ye'll never live t' see the day when even a stinkin' weed on it 'll belong t' ye!'

He says he hates her and leaves as Cabot enters. She tells him Eben has been mocking him and twists the conversation to the inheritance of the farm. She tells him Eben lusts after her and as he angers she backs off in her accusations. Reassured, he says that she can have the farm if she bears the son she says she wants with him. He says that he'd 'do anythin' ye axed, I tell ye!' if she gave him a son and tells her to pray to God for it to happen.

Scene Two

It is about eight in the evening and here the bedrooms are highlighted, with Eben in one and Cabot with Abbie in the other The two of them are talking about a son. They seem together, yet apart, as he tells her of his life on the farm and how God's hard He both lost and gained on the way through, but the farm is his. He says he is pleased he found her, his 'Rose o' Sharon'. Abbie promises him that she will bear a son as he basically threatens her,

> 'Ye don't know nothin' – nor never will. If ye don't hev a son t' redeem ye...'

and he leaves to sleep in the barn with the cows 'whar it's restful'.

We then see Eben and Abbie restless and she leaves the room and goes to him. He 'submits' to her kisses then 'hurls' her away. Abbie says she'd make him 'happy' and she knows he wants her too much. She tells him to go down to the parlour and he is shocked as this is where his mother was 'laid out'. She leaves for the parlour and he wonders what's happening. The scene closes with a question to his dead mother, 'Maw! Whar are yew?' but we know that he wants her and will go to her.

Scene Three

The scene now shifts to the parlour which is described as a 'grim, repressed room like a tomb'. Abbie waits and Eben appears and he sits at her invitation. They talk about his Maw and how they hate Cabot. Abbie throws herself at him with 'wild passion' and he is caught up in the moment and thinks that it's his Maw wanting him to sleep with Abbie to get revenge on Cabot,

I see it! I sees why. It's her vengeance on him – so's she
kin rest quiet in her grave!

Abbie proclaims her love for him and he for her then they kiss 'in
a fierce, bruising kiss' to close the scene.

Scene Four

A more bold and confident Eben leaves the house and Abbie opens
the parlour window. She calls him over for a kiss and they talk a
bit before Eben says his Maw can now rest. They split as Cabot
comes out of the barn but are now obviously in love. Eben tells
Cabot that his Maw is now at rest and Cabot says he rests best
with the cows. Cabot is confused but the scene ends with him
criticising Eben as 'Soft-headed' and a 'born fool' but, being a
practical man, he heads for breakfast.

Part Three: Scene One

Time has passed to 'late spring the following year'. Eben is upstairs
in emotional and psychological conflict while a party happens
downstairs. Cabot has drunk too much and Abbie sits, pale and
thin, in a rocking chair. There is a fiddler and Abbie begins the
scene by asking for Eben and the guests 'titter' as most think the
baby is Eben's, not Cabot's, which is true enough. They laugh and
Cabot is angered by this and orders them to dance. The fiddler
'slyly' says they're waiting for Eben but Cabot mocks the boy and
then ensues a bawdy conversation about his fertility,

I got a lot in me – a hell of a lot – folks don't know on.
Fiddle 'er up, durn ye! Give 'em somethin' t' dance t!'

The fiddler plays and they dance. Cabot joins in frantically and 'whoop(s)' it up. He exhausts the fiddler and pours whiskey. In the upstairs room Eben is looking at the baby. Abbie goes upstairs and Cabot leaves for outside, 'fresh air', as she has told him not to 'tech' her. The guests gossip after he goes and we see Eben and Abbie upstairs and she professes her love for him,

> 'Don't git feelin' low. I love ye, Eben. Kiss me.'

Cabot says he's going to rest in the barn. The scene concludes with the fiddler playing in celebration of 'the old skunk gittin fooled!'

Scene Two

Eben is outside half an hour later and Cabot is coming back from the barn. Cabot tells him to get a woman inside and he might get a farm. Eben replies that this farm's his and Cabot mocks him. He tells her Abbie has been promised the farm for her son and Eben is angered thinking Abbie has tricked him.

Eben goes to kill her but Cabot is too strong for him and Abbie comes out to stop him choking Eben. Cabot tells him he's weak and goes inside to celebrate. Abbie tries to be tender with Eben but he rejects her and calls her a liar.

> 'Ye're nothin' but a stinkin' passel o' lies. Ye've been lyin'
> t' me every word ye spoke, day an' night, since we fust –
> done it. Ye've kept sayin' ye loved me....'

She says she loves him and tells him that the promise was made before they fell in love. He says he'll go to California.

They argue and he 'torturedly' says he wished the baby had never been born. Abbie is distraught and she says she'd kill the baby to prove her love for him. He says he won't listen to her but she calls after him that she can 'prove' she loves him and she 'kin do one thin' God does'. Abbie is desperate at the end of the scene.

Scene Three

It is now just before dawn and Eben is in the kitchen ready to leave. Abbie is near the cradle with 'her face full of terror'. She sobs but Cabot stirs and she goes to the kitchen and flings her arms around Eben, kissing him 'wildly'. She says 'I killed him' and he thinks she means Cabot but is horrified when she tells him it's the baby.

Eben states it was his baby and she says she loved it but loves him more. He is angered,

> 'Don't ye tech me! Ye're pizzen! How could ye – t' murder
> a pore little critter – Ye must've swapped yer soul t' hell!

and tells her that he is getting the Sheriff and heads, 'panting and sobbing' to town. She calls out to him that she loves him.

Scene Four

It is after dawn and Abbie is in the kitchen. Cabot wakes in his room and is concerned that he has woken late. He checks the baby and is proud it is quiet and asleep. He goes down to Abbie in the kitchen and she tells him the baby is dead. He runs to check and comes back down and asks 'why?'

In a rage she tells him it was Eben's son and that she loves Eben not him. He blinks back a tear and then gets 'stony' so he can carry on and says he is going to get the Sheriff. Abbie tells him that Eben's already gone so that Cabot tells her he'll 'git t' wuk.' He then tells her he'd never have told and now he's going to be 'lonesomer'n ever!' Eben comes back and Cabot tells him to get off the farm.

Eben asks for her forgiveness and tells her he loves her. He says he realised he loved her at the Sheriff's and they have a chance to run away but Abbie says she'll take her punishment. Eben says he will share it with her and plans to tell the Sheriff they planned it together. They think they can stand it together and then Cabot comes back.

He goes into a long tirade and tells them how he's let the stock go and will burn the house down. He too plans to go to California but finds that Eben has gotten to his money first. Cabot says that this is a sign from God to him to stay and that 'God's hard an' lonesome!' At this point the Sheriff comes and Eben says he was involved with the baby's murder.

Cabot says 'Take 'em both' and leaves to get his stock. The sun is coming up and as they are led away Eben says the farm's 'Purty' and Abbie agrees. The Sheriff finishes the play with the line, 'It's a jim-dandy farm, no denyin'. Wish I owned it!'

OTHER RELATED TEXTS

Fiction / Non-fiction / Drama

- *Wonder* – R G Palacio
- *First they Killed My Father* – Luong Ung
- *The Graveyard Book* – Neil Gaiman
- *Looking for Alaska* – John Green
- *Eleanor and Park* by Rainbow Rowell
- *The Fault in Our Stars* – John Green
- *We All Fall Down* – Robert Cormier
- *The Old Man and the Sea* – Ernest Hemingway
- *The Fire Eaters* – David Almond
- *Ender's Game* – Orson Scott Card
- *Hatchet* – Gary Paulsen
- *Inside Black Australia* – Kevin Gilbert
- *Sapiens: A Brief History of Humankind* – Yuval Noah Harari
- *Peeling the Onion* – Wendy Orr
- *Raw* – Scott Monk
- *Six Degrees of Separation* – John Guare
- *The Book Thief* – Markus Zusak
- *When Dogs Cry* – Markus Zusak
- *Holes* – Louis Sachar
- *The Outsiders* – S.E. Hinton
- *Roll of Thunder, Hear My Cry* – Mildred D. Taylor
- *A Small Free Kiss in the Dark* – Glenda Millard
- *Monster* – Walter Dean Myers
- *Lord of the Flies* – William Golding
- *Jandamarra* – Steve Hawke
- *A Separate Peace* – John Knowles
- *A Monster Calls* – Patrick Ness
- *The Pigman* – Paul Zindel
- *The Invention of Hugo Cabret* – Brian Selznik

- *Emerald City* – David Williamson
- *Silent Spring* – Rachel Carson

Films and Television

- *The Human Experience* – Charles Kinnane
- *My Brilliant Career* – Gillian Armstrong
- *Broadchurch* – James Strong & Euros Lyn
- *Twinsters* – Samantha Futerman and Ryan Miyamoto
- *Be My Brother* – Genevieve Clay - Smith
- *What's Eating Gilbert Grape* – Lasse Hallstrom
- *Pleasantville* – Gary Ross
- *Eternal Sunshine of the Spotless Mind* – Michel Gondry
- *Taxi Driver* – Martin Scorsese
- *Tootsie* – Sydney Pollack
- *Back in Time for Dinner* – Kim Maddever
- *The Godfather* – Francis Ford Coppola
- *Friends* – David Crane and Marta Kaufmann
- *Dawson's Creek* – Kevin Williamson
- *Orange is the New Black* – Jenji Kohan
- *Boy Meets World* – Michael Jacobs and April Kelly

Website – quote on literature and the human experience

http://view2.fdu.edu/academics/university-college/school-of-humanities/
english-language-and-literature-program/

> At its most fundamental level literature explores what it means to be a human being in this world and tries to describe what our human experience is like. As such, literature pushes us to confront the large human questions that have plagued humankind for centuries: issues of fate and free will, issues relating to our role in the universe, our relationship to God, and our

relationships with others. Studying literature not only helps us to understand the complexity of these questions intellectually, but because of its very nature, it allows us to experience these tensions vicariously. Literature does not just tell us about human experience; it recreates it in a way we can feel and visualise. In other words, it calls for a total response from us—it stretches us beyond who we are.

First, literature can enhance our ability to relate to people. Because literature focuses on human relationships and self perception, it can broaden our own experience—to help us understand different kinds of people, different cultures, different problems—and, consequently, help us better understand our own relationships with others.

The study of literature also helps to foster an appreciation for beauty, symmetry, and order. This means more than the intuitive response of liking or disliking something we see or read or hear; it means a carefully thought-through response that will enhance appreciation—not destroy it.

Perhaps the most important skills that the study of literature teaches are analytic and synthetic skills. In learning to read carefully and analytically, we learn to ask hard questions both of the work and of ourselves. And as we seek to discover the relationships between the ideas and images we uncover in a work, our ultimate goal is to see the whole—to see how the parts work together to make the piece what it is. In grappling with the complex and difficult ideas contained in literature, we learn to accept the multiple dimensions and ambiguity that are so often present in life.

Finally, the study of literature will also help develop our writing abilities as we come to value the written word and understand its power to communicate.

Beyond all of these skills, however, it is not what literature can do for us as individuals as much as what it can do to us. Literature speaks to the whole person. Listen to it, says C. S. Lewis, and you will be changed.

Poetry

- 'Warren Pryor' – Alden Nowlan
- 'The Gardener' – Louis MacNeice
- 'The Improvers' – Colin Thiele

Songs

- *Be My Escape* – Relient K
- *Mandolin Wind* – Rod Stewart
- *Roxanne* – The Police
- *Wake Me Up When September Ends* – Green Day
- *Under Pressure* – Queen & David Bowie
- *Candle in the Wind* – Elton John
- *Empire State of Mind* – Alicia Keys
- *Gold Digger* – Kanye West
- *We Are Young* – Fun.
- *Centrefold* – J. Geils Band
- *It's Time* – Imagine Dragons
- *We Cry* – The Script
- *If I Were a Boy* – Beyoncé
- *Shake it Out* – Florence + the Machine
- *C'mon* – Panic! At the Disco & Fun.
- *I Don't Love You* – My Chemical Romance
- *Sing* – My Chemical Romance
- *1985* – Bowling for Soup
- *What About Me* – Shannon Noll
- *Sinner* – Jeremy Loops
- *7 Years* – Lucas Graham

- *Bitter Sweet Symphony* – The Verve
- *Ghost!* – Kid Kudi
- *Good Riddance (Time of Your Life)* – Green Day
- *Expectations* – Belle and Sebastian
- *After Hours* – We Are Scientists
- *Write About Love* – Belle and Sebastian
- *Trust Your Stomach* – Marching Band
- *Heaven Knows I'm Miserable Now* – The Smiths